The Ultimate Blackstone Griddle Recipe Book

A Blackstone Collection of Step-by-Step Recipes for Unforgettable Outdoor Occasions | Savor Perfect Steaks, Fluffy Eggs, Juicy Burgers, and More

Logan Tate

© Copyright 2025 by **Logan Tate** - All rights reserved.

This document is intended to provide accurate and reliable information on the subjects and facts covered.

- From a policy statement adopted and approved in equal parts by a committee of the American Bar Association and a committee of publishers and associations.

Reproduction, duplication or distribution of this document in electronic or printed form in any form is prohibited. All rights reserved.

The information contained herein is true and consistent, so any liability, in terms of carelessness or otherwise, arising from the use or misuse of the policies, procedures or **instructions** contained in this document is solely and entirely the responsibility of the recipient and reader. Under no circumstances shall the publisher be held liable or responsible for any recourse, damage or financial loss resulting directly or indirectly from the information contained herein.

All copyrights not owned by the publisher belong to the respective authors.

The information contained herein is provided for informational purposes only and as such is of general interest. The information is presented without contract or warranty of any kind.

Trademarks used are used without permission, and publication of the trademark is without permission or endorsement of the trademark owner. All trademarks and brands in this book are for illustrative purposes only and belong to the owners themselves, who are not associated with this document.

Table of Content

CHAPTER 1: INTRODUCTION TO THE BLACKSTONE GRIDDLE 8
- What is a Blackstone Griddle and Why Choose One? 8
- The Benefits of Cooking on a Griddle vs. a Traditional Grill 9
- Key Components and How They Work 10
- Structure, Materials, and Heat Management 11
- How to Distribute Heat for Optimal Cooking 12
- How to Properly Season Your Griddle and Why It Matters 14

CHAPTER 2: BASIC TECHNIQUES, MAINTENANCE, AND ESSENTIAL TOOLS 16
- Griddling, Searing, and Sautéing: When to Use Each Technique 16
- Controlling Temperature for Perfect Results 17
- Cleaning and Maintaining Your Griddle: Daily and Deep Cleaning Tips 18
- Must-Have Tools: Spatulas, Burger Press, Oils, and More 19

CHAPTER 3: GRILLED APPETIZERS & SNACKS 21
- *Liberty Bell Loaded Tater Tots* 21
- *Stars & Stripes Corn Fritters* 22
- *All-American Cheeseburger Sliders* 23
- *1776 Philly Cheesesteak Bites* 24
- *Frontier Campfire Queso Dip* 25
- *BBQ Rodeo Onion Rings* 26
- *Freedom Bacon-Wrapped Jalapeño Poppers* 27
- *Buffalo Soldier Chicken Bites* 28
- *Patriot Pretzel Bites with Beer Cheese* 29
- *Westward Ho' Grilled Cornbread Bites* 30
- *Smoky Uncle Sam Sausage Skewers* 31
- *Red, White & Blueberry Griddle Pancake Stacks* 32
- *Great Plains Griddled Cheese Curds* 33
- *Southern Glory Fried Pickle Chips* 34
- *The Founding Fathers' Fried Mac & Cheese Bites* 35

CHAPTER 4: FLAVORFUL VEGETABLES & SIDE DISHES 36
- *Liberty Skillet Corn with Honey Butter* 36
- *Stars & Stripes Sweet Potato Hash* 37
- *Frontier-Style Griddled Green Beans with Bacon* 38

The Founding Farmers' Homestyle Smashed Potatoes 39

Smoky Appalachian Grilled Brussels Sprouts 40

American Dream Cheesy Hash Browns 41

Westward Ho' Cowboy Baked Beans 42

Griddle-Seared Maple Glazed Carrots 43

Great Plains Garlic Butter Mushrooms 44

1776 Loaded Griddle Fries 45

Southern Glory Collard Greens & Cornbread Crumbles 46

Crispy Uncle Sam's Zucchini Fritters 47

Red, White & Blueberry Summer Slaw 48

Patriot-Style Fire-Roasted Peppers & Onions 49

All-American Griddled Mac & Cheese 50

CHAPTER 5: EASY MEAT RECIPES 51

Liberty Bell Griddle-Seared Ribeye 51

1776 Maple-Glazed Pork Chops 52

Frontier-Style Cowboy Steak Bites 53

Stars & Stripes Honey BBQ Chicken Thighs 54

All-American Griddled Meatloaf Patties 55

Buffalo Soldier Spicy Chicken Tenders 56

Uncle Sam's Smoked Sausage & Peppers 57

Southern Glory Country-Fried Steak 58

Westward Ho' Garlic Butter Pork Medallions 59

Great Plains Griddled Turkey Cutlets with Herb Butter 60

Freedom Sizzling Lamb Chops 61

Founding Fathers' Bourbon-Glazed Chicken Breasts 62

American Dream BBQ Pulled Pork Smash 63

Patriot-Style Teriyaki Beef Tips 64

Smoky Appalachian Griddle-Seared Ham Slices 65

Crispy Liberty Fried Chicken Cutlets 66

Red, White & Blueberry-Glazed Pork Ribs 67

Firecracker Cajun-Spiced Chicken Wings 68

Homestyle Blackstone Griddled Meatballs 69

Texas Trail Smoked Brisket Slices 70

CHAPTER 6: GRILLED FISH & SEAFOOD 71

Liberty Bell Lemon Butter Salmon Fillets 71

Stars & Stripes Cajun Shrimp Skewers 72

1776 Garlic Butter Lobster Tails 73

Frontier-Style Blackened Catfish 74

Smoky Appalachian Cedar-Plank Trout 75

Uncle Sam's Classic Fish & Chips 76

Great Plains Honey-Glazed Grilled Tilapia 77

American Dream Bourbon-Butter Scallops 78

Buffalo Soldier Spicy Shrimp Tacos 79

Southern Glory Crispy Cornmeal Fried Fish 80

Westward Ho' Griddled Garlic Butter Clams 81

The Founding Fathers' Seafood Paella Skillet 82

Freedom Firecracker Grilled Mahi-Mahi 83

Patriot-Style Old Bay Crab Cakes 84

Red, White & Blueberry-Glazed Salmon Steaks 85

Texas Trail Chili-Lime Shrimp Fajitas 86

Homestyle Blackstone Griddled Swordfish Steaks 87

Smoky BBQ Bacon-Wrapped Scallops 88

Fire-Roasted Garlic Parmesan Oysters 89

New England-Style Lobster Roll Sliders 90

CHAPTER 7: BURGERS & GOURMET SANDWICHES 91

Liberty Bell Classic Smash Burger 91

Stars & Stripes Bacon Cheddar BBQ Burger 92

1776 All-American Patty Melt 93

Frontier-Style Bison Burger with Caramelized Onions 94

Smoky Appalachian Pulled Pork Sandwich 95

Uncle Sam's Philly Cheesesteak Hoagie 96

Great Plains Juicy Lucy Stuffed Burger 97

American Dream Fried Chicken Sandwich 98

Buffalo Soldier Spicy Chicken Ranch Burger 99

Southern Glory Buttermilk Biscuit Sausage Sandwich 100

Westward Ho' BBQ Brisket Sliders 101

The Founding Fathers' Classic Reuben 102

Freedom Fire-Grilled Turkey Club 103

Patriot-Style Triple-Decker Grilled Cheese 104

Red, White & Blueberry BBQ Pulled Chicken Sandwich 105

CHAPTER 8: RECIPES FOR SPECIAL OCCASIONS 106

Liberty Bell New Year's Eve Surf & Turf Platter 106

Stars & Stripes Fourth of July BBQ Ribs 107

1776 Thanksgiving Griddled Turkey & Cranberry Sliders 108

Frontier-Style Cowboy Christmas Prime Rib 109

Smoky Appalachian Easter Honey-Glazed Ham 110

Uncle Sam's Memorial Day All-American Hot Dogs 111

Great Plains Father's Day Bourbon-Glazed Steak 112

American Dream Mother's Day Strawberry Shortcake Pancakes 113

Buffalo Soldier Super Bowl Buffalo Chicken Nachos 114

Southern Glory Mardi Gras Cajun Shrimp & Grits 115

Westward Ho' Halloween Spooky Smash Burgers 116

The Founding Fathers' Labor Day Grilled Sausage & Peppers 117

Freedom Christmas Eve Griddled Seafood Feast 118

Patriot-Style Veteran's Day Smoked Brisket Plate 119

Red, White & Blueberry 4th of July Flag Cake 120

CHAPTER 9: ADVANCED TIPS & TRICKS 121

HOW TO GET THE PERFECT CRISP ON EVERYTHING 121

SPICE COMBINATIONS TO ELEVATE EVERY DISH 122

TECHNIQUES FOR EVEN COOKING & AVOIDING BURNT FOOD 123

CHAPTER 10: MEASUREMENT CONVERSIONS 125

U.S. TO METRIC UNIT CONVERSIONS 125

TEMPERATURE CONVERSION CHART (FAHRENHEIT TO CELSIUS) 125

WEIGHT & VOLUME EQUIVALENTS: TABLESPOONS TO OUNCES & GRAMS 126

CONCLUSION 127

YOUR BLACKSTONE JOURNEY: WHAT YOU'VE LEARNED 127

HOW TO KEEP IMPROVING YOUR GRIDDLE SKILLS 128

EXCLUSIVE BONUS MATERIALS

Unlock the full potential of your Blackstone Griddle with these specially crafted bonus materials, each designed to enhance your outdoor cooking experience:

🔥 BONUS 1: "Griddle Gourmet Video Series"
Dive into the world of outdoor grilling with this exclusive video series. Discover techniques that combine your favorite recipes with the unique capabilities of the Blackstone Griddle, perfect for any social gathering or backyard feast.

🔥 BONUS 2: "Ultimate Griddle Care Handbook"
Maintain your griddle like a pro with this comprehensive PDF guide. Learn everything from basic cleaning to advanced maintenance, making it easier than ever to enjoy your griddle for years to come.

🔥 BONUS 3: "Four Seasons Griddle Recipe Planner"
Stay inspired all year round with seasonal recipe updates delivered directly to your inbox. Each season, you'll receive new recipes that are perfect for any outdoor occasion, ensuring you never run out of ideas for using your Blackstone Griddle.

🔥 Scan the QR code now to access your personalized resources and start transforming the way you grill outdoors!

CHAPTER 1: INTRODUCTION TO THE BLACKSTONE GRIDDLE

A Blackstone Griddle isn't just another piece of outdoor cooking equipment—it's a tool that redefines how food is cooked. Built for precision, power, and versatility, it delivers a level of control that traditional grills can't match. From its solid steel surface to its independent burners, every component is designed to create an unmatched cooking experience. Understanding how it works, how heat moves across its surface, and how to properly season it transforms a simple flat-top into a high-performance kitchen that lasts for years.

What is a Blackstone Griddle and Why Choose One?

The **Blackstone Griddle** is not just another piece of outdoor cooking equipment—it's a game-changer. Unlike traditional grills that rely on open flames and grates, a Blackstone Griddle is a **flat-top cooking surface** made of high-quality cold-rolled steel, designed to provide **consistent, even heating** across a large area. It's an evolution of the **teppanyaki-style grills** used in Japanese cuisine and the diner griddles found in classic American roadside restaurants. What makes it stand out? **Versatility, efficiency, and sheer cooking power.**

At first glance, it might look like just a large, flat slab of metal sitting atop a burner system, but the magic lies in what it can do. A standard gas grill has **hot spots and flare-ups**, making precise cooking difficult. A Blackstone Griddle eliminates that problem by providing **direct contact between the food and the heated surface**, ensuring a **consistent sear** while locking in moisture. With traditional grills, juices drip through the grates, often causing flare-ups or losing flavor. On a griddle, those juices stay where they belong—infusing the food with richness and depth.

The **cooking surface is expansive**, offering plenty of room to cook multiple items at once. You're no longer limited to grilling just burgers and steaks. The Blackstone can handle **pancakes, eggs, bacon, stir-fries, fajitas, cheesesteaks, fried rice, smash burgers, and even delicate items like flaky fish and crepes.** You can sauté vegetables, toast buns, and sear meat—all at the same time—without juggling multiple pans or worrying about food falling through the grates.

A major advantage of a Blackstone Griddle is **temperature control**. Gas grills often struggle with inconsistent heat distribution, especially when the lid is up. The Blackstone's design ensures **uniform heat spread**, allowing you to create **temperature zones**—one side for high-heat searing, another for keeping food warm or slow-cooking delicate items. This level of control gives you **restaurant-quality results** in an outdoor setting.

Durability is another selling point. Blackstone griddles are **built for longevity**, crafted from **cold-rolled steel**—a material prized for its strength and heat retention. Over time, as you season the griddle, it develops a **non-stick surface**, similar to cast iron, that only gets better with use. While other grills can suffer from rusted-out grates or deteriorating burners, a well-maintained Blackstone is an investment that can last for decades.

Of course, no cooking method is without its limitations. The Blackstone requires **regular seasoning and maintenance** to prevent rust and maintain its non-stick properties. It also lacks the traditional smoky flavor that a charcoal grill provides, though that can be mitigated by using **smoked salts, wood-chip smoker boxes, or liquid smoke-infused marinades**.

For those who love **bold flavors, high-heat searing, and the ability to cook just about anything**, a Blackstone Griddle isn't just a cooking tool—it's a **kitchen revolution** that brings the experience of a diner, a hibachi grill, and a backyard BBQ together in one powerhouse of a machine.

The Benefits of Cooking on a Griddle vs. a Traditional Grill

Cooking isn't just about throwing food on a heat source and hoping for the best. The method you choose determines the **flavor, texture, and overall quality** of your meal. Traditional grills have dominated American backyards for decades, but a griddle offers a **fundamentally different cooking experience**, one that's often superior depending on what's on the menu.

A Blackstone griddle is **a continuous, flat cooking surface**, which means **no gaps, no grates, and no risk of food slipping through the cracks**. This alone makes it **far more efficient** for cooking smaller or delicate items—things like scrambled eggs, sliced onions, diced potatoes, or shrimp, which would be nearly impossible to cook properly on an open grill without a cast iron pan.

Heat distribution is another game changer. A traditional grill creates **hot spots and cool zones**, which means half of your food might be overcooked while the other half is still struggling to warm up. A griddle's surface **spreads heat evenly**, allowing for **precise temperature control across different areas**. You can sear a steak at high heat on one side while gently cooking vegetables on the other. The flexibility this provides is unmatched.

One of the biggest drawbacks of traditional grills is **flare-ups**. When fat drips onto an open flame, it creates sudden bursts of fire, leading to **uneven cooking, charring, and even dangerous situations** if not managed carefully. A griddle eliminates this issue entirely. Since there are no open flames directly under the food, everything **cooks consistently**, with no unexpected flare-ups burning one side of your burger while leaving the inside raw.

The moisture retention on a griddle is another major advantage. When you grill a burger or a piece of chicken on a traditional grill, **the juices drip away, disappearing into the flames below**. That's wasted flavor, gone before it ever has a chance to enhance your food. On a griddle, **those juices stay on the surface**, allowing the food to reabsorb its own moisture, leading to **juicier, more flavorful bites**. This is why smash burgers, when cooked on a griddle, have such an **incredible crust while still being ultra-juicy inside**—something that's almost impossible to achieve on a traditional grill.

A griddle also excels at **versatility**. While a standard grill is fantastic for steaks and hot dogs, it's **limited in what it can do**. A griddle, on the other hand, **expands your cooking possibilities exponentially**. Breakfast favorites like bacon, pancakes, and hash browns? No problem. Stir-fried dishes, quesadillas, grilled cheese sandwiches? Effortless. Even cooking techniques like sautéing or caramelizing are fair game, turning the Blackstone into **a fully functional outdoor kitchen**.

That's not to say a griddle is perfect for everything. If you want **that signature smoky, wood-fired taste**, a traditional grill still has its place. But when it comes to **control, versatility, and efficiency**, a griddle isn't just an alternative—it's an upgrade.

Key Components and How They Work

The **Blackstone Griddle** isn't just a big flat slab of metal with burners underneath. It's a carefully engineered cooking system designed for **precision, efficiency, and durability**. Every part of it—from the surface to the ignition system—plays a role in delivering the **searing power, even heat distribution, and versatility** that makes it a **staple for backyard cooks and professional chefs alike**.

The **griddle top** is the heart of the Blackstone. It's made from **cold-rolled steel**, a material chosen for its **exceptional heat retention and durability**. Unlike stainless steel, which can develop hot spots and lose heat quickly, cold-rolled steel **distributes heat evenly** and **maintains temperature** even when cooking large amounts of food. Over time, this surface develops a **natural non-stick patina** through seasoning, which enhances performance and prevents food from sticking. But there's a catch—**it requires regular maintenance**. If left exposed to moisture, it can rust, and if not seasoned properly, food will stick and burn.

Underneath the griddle top sits the **burner system**, the powerhouse of the entire setup. Depending on the model, a Blackstone Griddle is equipped with **two to four independent burners**, each connected to a **propane fuel source**. These burners are designed to provide **direct, controllable heat** to different zones of the cooking surface, allowing you to cook at multiple temperatures at the same time. Unlike traditional gas grills, which rely on open flames to char food, the Blackstone's burners heat the steel directly, eliminating flare-ups and ensuring a **consistent cooking environment**.

Ignition is another critical element. Blackstone uses a **push-button piezo ignition system**, a **spark-based mechanism** that lights the burners instantly with the turn of a knob. Some higher-end models even feature **electronic ignition systems**, which offer **more reliability and less wear over time**. While these systems are generally dependable, they can fail if exposed to grease buildup or moisture, requiring occasional cleaning or replacement.

The **grease management system** is another defining feature. Traditional grills force you to battle flare-ups from dripping fat, but the Blackstone is built with an **angled grease flow system** that directs excess oils and food particles into a removable grease trap. This **keeps the cooking surface clean**, reduces smoke, and prevents grease fires. However, if not emptied regularly, grease can overflow or clog the system, creating a mess and affecting performance.

The **frame and cart assembly** complete the design, providing stability and portability. Most Blackstone models come with **sturdy steel frames, side shelves, and wheels for mobility**, allowing for easy outdoor setup. Some versions even include **built-in storage, foldable legs, and wind guards**, making them adaptable to different cooking environments.

Every component of the Blackstone Griddle is built for **high-performance outdoor cooking**, but like any professional-grade tool, it requires proper use and upkeep. Understanding how each part works isn't just about knowing the equipment—it's about **getting the most out of every meal**.

Structure, Materials, and Heat Management

A Blackstone Griddle isn't just a simple flat-top cooking surface—it's a precision-built machine designed to **handle extreme heat, distribute it evenly, and maintain it efficiently**. Every element of its construction, from the type of steel used to the design of the burners, plays a role in how it performs. Understanding how these components interact is the key to maximizing its potential.

At the core of the griddle's structure is its **cold-rolled steel cooking surface**, a material chosen for its **superior heat retention and durability**. Unlike standard stainless steel, which is prone to uneven heating, cold-rolled steel ensures **a more consistent temperature across the surface**, reducing the risk of burning one side of your food while the other side struggles to cook. This steel undergoes a compression process that enhances its **density and smoothness**, allowing for more direct heat transfer and a **naturally developing non-stick patina** over time. While this makes for an excellent cooking experience, it also requires care—if exposed to moisture or left unseasoned, the surface can oxidize and develop rust.

Beneath the griddle top, the **burner system** serves as the engine driving its performance. Depending on the model, the Blackstone is equipped with **multiple independent burners**, each designed to heat a specific section of the surface. Unlike traditional gas grills that rely on a singular heat source, these burners function independently, allowing for **temperature zones**—one area can be set to high heat for searing, while another remains at a lower setting for warming or delicate cooking. The precision this provides is crucial for achieving **restaurant-quality results**.

The material of the burners themselves matters as well. High-performance models utilize **stainless steel burners**, which offer **resistance to corrosion and long-term durability** even when exposed to grease, high heat, and the elements. Lower-end models may use cast iron burners, which, while efficient in heat retention, require more frequent maintenance to prevent clogging and rusting.

A key element in the overall efficiency of the Blackstone Griddle is **heat distribution**. Unlike an open-flame grill where food is suspended above flames, the Blackstone applies **direct heat contact** across the entire cooking surface. This eliminates the unpredictable nature of traditional grilling, where food placement is critical due to uneven flames. The controlled flow of heat allows for more precise cooking, but it also introduces a responsibility—the surface must be **preheated correctly** to ensure uniform heat spread. If one section is hotter than another, food can cook at different rates, making it essential to understand how your specific model retains and distributes energy.

Beyond heat distribution, the griddle's **frame and insulation** play a significant role in how well it performs outdoors. The supporting structure is built from **powder-coated steel**, which resists rust and provides stability. Some models come with **wind guards** to prevent heat loss, a factor that can drastically affect cooking times in breezy conditions. A lack of wind protection can lead to **temperature fluctuations**, making it difficult to achieve even browning and consistent cooking.

Every material and design choice in a Blackstone Griddle is intentional, built to **maximize heat efficiency, maintain durability, and provide an adaptable cooking experience**. Knowing how these components work together isn't just about understanding your equipment—it's about using it to its full potential.

How to Distribute Heat for Optimal Cooking

Mastering heat distribution on a **Blackstone Griddle** isn't just about turning the burners on and hoping for the best. This flat-top cooking surface demands a deeper understanding of **how heat moves, how different zones develop, and how to manipulate those variables** for the best results. Precision matters. Without it, you'll find yourself frustrated by food that burns on one side while staying undercooked on the other.

Unlike a traditional grill where food is cooked by direct flames, a griddle uses **conductive heat transfer**. The burners underneath heat the cold-rolled steel, which then distributes that energy across the surface. However, the steel doesn't heat perfectly evenly on its own. Some areas will run hotter than others due to burner placement, external factors like wind, and the simple physics of metal expansion. This is why understanding **heat zones** is critical to getting consistently great food off the griddle.

The griddle's layout naturally creates different **temperature zones**, and learning how to use them effectively will separate an amateur from a true griddle master. The section directly above a burner will always be the hottest, perfect for searing meats, caramelizing onions, or achieving a deep, golden-brown crust on smash burgers. Moving a few inches away, you'll find a moderate heat zone—ideal for foods that require steady cooking without excessive charring, like eggs, pancakes, or stir-fried vegetables. The farthest edges of the griddle, particularly corners, tend to be the coolest, making them perfect for **keeping food warm without overcooking it**.

A common mistake beginners make is trying to cook everything at the same temperature. This leads to meals that are either **overcooked in some areas and underdone in others or require unnecessary flipping and moving around**. The best approach is to **intentionally create heat zones** by controlling burner output. Keeping one side on high and another on low lets you manage multiple cooking tasks simultaneously. If you're making breakfast, bacon can crisp up in the high-heat area while hash browns slowly develop their golden crust in a medium zone, and scrambled eggs can finish gently in a lower heat section without becoming rubbery.

Wind and outdoor temperature can also impact how heat spreads across the griddle. In colder conditions, heat retention becomes a challenge, and exposed flame areas may struggle to keep the surface evenly hot. Some griddle users invest in **wind guards** to combat this issue, preventing heat loss and ensuring steady cooking temperatures. Another key factor is **preheating**. A Blackstone Griddle needs time to **reach and stabilize its optimal temperature**, which can take anywhere from **5 to 15 minutes** depending on the size and outdoor conditions. Skipping this step leads to uneven heat and unpredictable cooking times.

Keeping the cooking surface properly maintained also influences heat distribution. A well-seasoned griddle conducts heat more efficiently than one with uneven layers of seasoning or built-up food debris. If the surface is patchy, areas with thick carbonized buildup can act as **insulators**, reducing direct heat transfer and causing unpredictable hot and cold spots.

Perfecting heat control isn't about guessing—it's about **reading the surface, understanding burner placement, and adjusting as you go**. The more you cook, the more second nature it becomes, turning your Blackstone Griddle into a **precision cooking tool rather than just a hot piece of metal**.

How to Properly Season Your Griddle and Why It Matters

A **Blackstone Griddle** is not ready to cook on straight out of the box. That pristine, smooth steel surface may look good, but it lacks the protective barrier needed for proper performance. **Seasoning** is the process of bonding **thin layers of oil to the metal surface through heat, creating a durable, non-stick cooking area that improves with use**. Skipping this step or doing it incorrectly will lead to food sticking, uneven cooking, and worse—rust that can destroy the griddle's lifespan.

The seasoning process starts with a **completely clean griddle**. Any factory coatings must be burned off, and the surface must be wiped down to remove any manufacturing residues. Once dry, a **thin layer of high-smoke point oil**—such as flaxseed, canola, or avocado oil—is applied across the entire surface, including the sides and edges. The griddle is then heated until the oil smokes and bonds with the metal, a process known as **polymerization**. This step is repeated multiple times to build a **protective, non-stick layer** that strengthens with every cook.

A proper seasoning does more than prevent food from sticking. It acts as a **barrier against oxidation**, preventing moisture from reaching the steel. Without it, even the slightest exposure to humidity or rain can lead to rust, which eats away at the cooking surface. A well-seasoned griddle is not just functional—it's practically self-cleaning. Food releases more easily, requiring only a light scrape and a wipe-down after use, rather than heavy scrubbing.

The biggest mistake people make when seasoning is applying **too much oil at once**. If the layer is too thick, it will not polymerize properly, leaving behind a **sticky, uneven surface** rather than the hard, smooth coating needed for high-heat cooking. Each application should be so thin that it barely looks like anything is there. The goal is to build up multiple microscopic layers rather than one thick coat.

Heat distribution plays a role in how seasoning bonds. If the burners are not heating evenly, some areas may polymerize faster than others, leading to **patchy seasoning**. Over time, regular cooking will help even out these inconsistencies, but the initial layers should be applied carefully to create a uniform base.

A new griddle will often develop a **dark, almost bronze-like hue** after the first few seasoning cycles. This is completely normal and a sign that the oil is bonding correctly. With continued use, the surface will gradually turn **a deep, glossy black**, which indicates a well-developed seasoning. This evolution is part of what makes the Blackstone Griddle unique—every griddle takes on its own character over time, shaped by the way it's used.

If the seasoning ever starts to degrade, whether from cooking acidic foods, using too much water to clean, or exposure to moisture, it can be restored. A light reapplication of oil after each use helps maintain the integrity of the surface, while a full re-seasoning can bring a neglected griddle back to life. A properly seasoned Blackstone is an investment that **pays off in performance, longevity, and flavor**, turning a simple steel plate into a **cooking powerhouse**.

CHAPTER 2: BASIC TECHNIQUES, MAINTENANCE, AND ESSENTIAL TOOLS

Cooking on a **Blackstone Griddle** is more than just heating up a flat surface—it's about mastering techniques, controlling temperature, and maintaining the griddle to keep it performing at its best. Whether it's knowing when to sear, griddle, or sauté, keeping the surface properly seasoned, or using the right tools for the job, each step plays a role in delivering flawless results every time.

Griddling, Searing, and Sautéing: When to Use Each Technique

Cooking on a Blackstone Griddle isn't just about turning up the heat and tossing food onto the surface. Every ingredient reacts differently depending on temperature, oil content, and cooking time, making **technique** just as important as the tools being used. Three primary methods—**griddling, searing, and sautéing**—define how heat interacts with food, determining texture, moisture retention, and overall flavor. Each has its place, but knowing when and how to use them is what separates a casual backyard cook from someone who truly understands the potential of a flat-top griddle.

Griddling is the foundation of cooking on a Blackstone. This technique relies on moderate, **even heat applied across the entire cooking surface**, allowing foods to develop a golden-brown crust without excessive charring. It's ideal for **smash burgers, breakfast staples like pancakes and bacon, grilled sandwiches, and even vegetables that need slow caramelization**. The beauty of this method is in its ability to **lock in moisture while building flavor**, a direct result of consistent heat application. Because there are no open flames, foods cook in their own rendered fat or cooking oil, amplifying depth without drying out. Unlike a traditional grill, where drippings are lost to the fire, a griddle **retains every bit of flavor**, making it a superior choice for foods that benefit from their own juices.

Searing, on the other hand, is a high-heat technique used to create **a deep, flavorful crust on proteins like steak, pork chops, and thick-cut chicken breast**. This process relies on the **Maillard reaction**, a chemical transformation that occurs when amino acids and sugars in food brown under extreme heat. A proper sear requires a **preheated surface**, an oil with a high smoke point, and minimal movement of the food until the crust has formed. The mistake most people make is flipping too soon, preventing the sear from fully developing. A properly seared steak will have a **dark, almost crispy crust** that locks in moisture, while a rushed one will look pale and lifeless. Timing and patience define this method. If the temperature is too low, food steams instead of sears. If it's too high, the outside burns before the inside cooks. The right balance depends on the cut and thickness of the protein, but once mastered, this technique transforms the griddle into a **steakhouse-level cooking surface**.

Sautéing is about movement and precision, best suited for **smaller, quick-cooking ingredients like diced vegetables, shrimp, and thinly sliced meats**. Unlike griddling and searing, which rely on constant surface contact, sautéing uses **rapid motion to distribute heat evenly** while preventing overcooking. The key is using just enough oil to **coat the food without drowning it**, combined with the right amount of heat to create a light char while keeping the interior tender. Since a Blackstone lacks the sloped edges of a traditional sauté pan, spatula work becomes essential, allowing food to be **flipped, tossed, and moved efficiently**. This method excels in stir-fries, fajitas, and anything requiring a **quick, high-heat cook without sacrificing texture or flavor**.

Each of these techniques plays a distinct role in maximizing what a Blackstone Griddle can do. Whether building layers of flavor in a slow-griddled dish, locking in juices with a hard sear, or rapidly developing caramelization through sautéing, the key to success is **understanding heat control and how food reacts to it**.

Controlling Temperature for Perfect Results

Cooking on a **Blackstone Griddle** is all about **heat management**. The burners beneath the steel surface may look straightforward, but controlling them correctly determines whether a meal turns out flawlessly cooked or frustratingly uneven. The **griddle top doesn't react instantly** the way a pan on a stovetop would. Heat builds up, distributes, and lingers, making **temperature control an active process rather than a simple adjustment of a knob**.

A Blackstone operates on **direct conductive heat**, meaning the surface itself is responsible for cooking, not an open flame. That changes how food reacts. Proteins, starches, and vegetables all respond differently depending on the intensity of the heat beneath them. A steak needs a **blazing hot zone** to develop a rich crust without overcooking inside. Eggs, on the other hand, require a **gentle low heat** to avoid turning rubbery. Because the griddle provides a large, continuous surface, its most powerful advantage is the ability to **create different temperature zones simultaneously**.

Heat zones develop naturally based on burner placement. The area directly above a lit burner is always the hottest. Moving a few inches away, the heat gradually lowers, providing a **gradient of cooking temperatures**. This layout allows for **searing, browning, and warming—all at the same time**. A properly used griddle never forces food to cook at a single, universal heat level. Instead, it provides **hot zones for rapid searing, medium zones for steady cooking, and cooler areas for holding or finishing**.

Understanding how long heat takes to transfer is just as critical. Unlike a stovetop, where a pan changes temperature within seconds, a Blackstone retains and **radiates** heat even after the burner is turned down. A sudden temperature drop won't immediately affect the surface, which means **adjustments need to be anticipated**. Preheating is also non-negotiable. The steel requires **at least 5 to 10 minutes** to reach a stable cooking temperature. A cold griddle produces weak, inconsistent results, preventing food from developing the correct texture.

Cooking techniques depend on these heat dynamics. Smash burgers demand a **scorching hot surface** to create the perfect Maillard crust. Pancakes need even, medium heat to develop golden brown exteriors without burning. Vegetables that contain a lot of water cook better with **controlled heat**, preventing them from turning mushy before they caramelize. A griddle is not just a **flat pan**—it's a surface that rewards **patience and knowledge of how heat moves**.

Wind, humidity, and outdoor temperatures also impact performance. Wind strips away heat from the surface, requiring **higher burner settings to compensate**. Cold weather forces the steel to **work harder to maintain its temperature**, demanding longer preheating times. Griddle users who overlook these factors often end up struggling with **inconsistent cooking results**.

Mastering temperature control isn't just about watching the flame—it's about knowing how heat **builds, spreads, and interacts with food**. A Blackstone isn't just a cooking tool, it's a **thermal landscape** that must be **understood and adjusted in real-time** for flawless execution.

Cleaning and Maintaining Your Griddle: Daily and Deep Cleaning Tips

A **Blackstone Griddle** isn't like a nonstick pan you can toss in the sink and scrub down with soapy water. It's a **seasoned steel cooking surface** that needs specific care to maintain its non-stick properties, prevent rust, and ensure consistent performance over time. The way a griddle is cleaned and maintained after each use directly impacts its **longevity, heat distribution, and cooking results**. A well-kept griddle lasts for decades. A neglected one turns into a patchy, rusted, uneven mess that can ruin food and require resurfacing.

Daily cleaning starts the moment cooking is finished. While the griddle is still warm—but not scalding hot—any excess food particles and grease should be scraped off using a **flat-edge metal spatula or a griddle scraper**. Leftover bits of food will harden as the griddle cools, making them significantly harder to remove later. The cooking surface should then be wiped down with a **dry paper towel or a cloth** to soak up any remaining oil and residue. A light coat of **neutral, high-smoke point oil** should be applied to the surface while it's still warm, ensuring the seasoning remains intact and the steel is protected from moisture.

What shouldn't be used is just as important. **Dish soap, steel wool, and abrasive cleaners are the enemy of a properly seasoned griddle.** Soap strips away the polymerized layers of oil that form the griddle's natural non-stick coating, and abrasive tools can create uneven surfaces that affect heat retention. Water should also be minimized. While a damp paper towel can help lift stubborn bits of food, excessive moisture left on the surface can quickly lead to rust, even if the griddle is stored indoors.

Deep cleaning is necessary when the griddle surface starts showing signs of buildup that affect cooking performance—like sticky residue, uneven dark spots, or excessive carbon layers that prevent food from making direct contact with the metal. Unlike daily maintenance, deep cleaning requires more effort but is essential for **restoring the surface to peak condition**. The best approach is to heat the griddle slightly, allowing hardened grease and food particles to loosen. A **griddle stone or grill brick** can then be used to gently scrub the surface, removing debris without damaging the seasoning. If needed, a **small amount of water** can be added to create steam that helps break down buildup, but it must be completely dried and re-oiled immediately afterward.

One of the biggest threats to any griddle is rust. Even a small amount of moisture left on the surface overnight can cause oxidation. If rust does appear, it should be removed immediately with **fine-grit sandpaper or steel wool**, followed by a full re-seasoning process to restore the protective layer.

Storage plays a role in maintenance as well. A griddle should never be left exposed to rain, humidity, or extreme temperature shifts. A **fitted cover** helps prevent dust and moisture accumulation, and for long-term storage, an additional layer of oil creates a protective barrier.

A well-maintained Blackstone doesn't just last—it **cooks better with every use**. Seasoning gets stronger, heat distribution improves, and the surface becomes smoother over time. Proper cleaning isn't just about keeping it looking good; it's about preserving the **performance and integrity of a cooking tool built to last.**

Must-Have Tools: Spatulas, Burger Press, Oils, and More

Cooking on a **Blackstone Griddle** isn't just about having the right ingredients—it's about having the right tools to handle them. Unlike a standard grill, where tongs and a basting brush might be all you need, a griddle requires **specialized equipment** that allows for **precise control, efficient movement, and optimal cooking performance**. Without the right tools, food sticks, heat distribution suffers, and results become inconsistent. Investing in the right gear transforms griddling from a basic outdoor activity into a **high-performance cooking experience**.

The spatula is the most essential tool, but not just any spatula will do. A griddle spatula needs to be **wide, sturdy, and slightly flexible**, capable of sliding underneath delicate foods like eggs while also being strong enough to handle a heavy smash burger. A **long, flat edge** is necessary for proper searing, ensuring that food makes full contact with the surface when flipped. Cheap, flimsy spatulas won't cut it—they lack the weight and balance needed to control food efficiently. Stainless steel models with a comfortable, heat-resistant grip work best, giving the control needed for **quick flips, smooth movements, and precise scraping**.

A **burger press** is non-negotiable for anyone serious about making the perfect smash burger. Applying **consistent, even pressure** to ground beef is what creates the signature **deep, golden crust** that defines a great griddle burger. A weighted press also works for **flattening bacon, pressing panini-style sandwiches, and ensuring even heat distribution**. Without it, food cooks inconsistently, losing the **caramelization and texture** that sets griddle cooking apart.

Using the right **oils** is just as important as having the right tools. Not all oils perform the same on a Blackstone. A good griddle oil needs a **high smoke point** to withstand the intense heat without breaking down. Canola, avocado, and grapeseed oil all work well for daily cooking, while **flaxseed oil is the best choice for seasoning**. Avoid butter alone—it burns too quickly, leaving behind sticky residues that degrade the non-stick properties of the griddle over time. Instead, butter should be combined with oil or added at the last stage of cooking for flavor.

A **griddle scraper** is essential for maintaining the cooking surface after every session. Unlike a standard grill, which allows residue to burn off between uses, a griddle needs to be **scraped clean while still warm** to prevent buildup from hardening. A scraper with a **sharp edge** removes food debris efficiently without damaging the seasoning, keeping the surface smooth and **ready for the next cook**.

Other small but critical tools include **squeeze bottles for oil and water**, allowing for controlled application without making a mess. Oil bottles ensure **an even, thin coating across the surface**, preventing food from sticking, while water bottles are used for **steam cooking, deglazing, and quick surface cooling** when adjusting heat zones. A **dome cover** is another game-changer, trapping heat and moisture for melting cheese, steaming vegetables, and cooking foods that need indirect heat without overcooking the exterior.

Precision, maintenance, and technique define the difference between an average griddle cook and someone who consistently produces restaurant-quality food. The way heat is controlled, the surface is cared for, and the right tools are used all impact the outcome. A well-maintained griddle, combined with proper cooking methods, doesn't just last—it gets better with every use.

CHAPTER 3: GRILLED APPETIZERS & SNACKS

Liberty Bell Loaded Tater Tots

Prep Time: 10 minutes | **Cook Time:** 15 minutes | **Total Time:** 25 minutes

Ingredients
Main Ingredients:
- 2 cups frozen tater tots
- ½ cup shredded sharp cheddar cheese
- 2 slices crispy bacon, crumbled
- ¼ cup diced scallions

Seasonings & Sauces:
- ½ teaspoon smoked paprika
- ¼ teaspoon garlic powder
- ¼ teaspoon onion powder
- 2 tablespoons sour cream
- 1 tablespoon BBQ sauce

Optional Additions:
- ¼ cup diced jalapeños
- 1 tablespoon chopped cilantro

Nutritional Information
- **Calories:** 420 kcal
- **Carbs:** 45g
- **Fiber:** 4g
- **Protein:** 12g
- **Fats:** 22g
- **Sugar:** 3g

Instructions
1. **Preheat the Blackstone Griddle** to **medium heat** and lightly oil the surface.
2. Spread tater tots on the griddle, cooking for **10–12 minutes**, flipping occasionally.
3. Sprinkle smoked paprika, garlic powder, and onion powder while cooking.
4. Reduce heat to **low**, add cheese, and cover with a dome for **1–2 minutes** to melt.
5. Remove from heat, top with bacon, scallions, BBQ sauce, and sour cream.

Chef's Tips: Use a spatula to press tots slightly for extra crunch.
Notes: Cook in batches to prevent overcrowding.

Stars & Stripes Corn Fritters

Prep Time: 15 minutes | **Cook Time:** 10 minutes | **Total Time:** 25 minutes

Ingredients
Main Ingredients:
- 1 cup fresh corn kernels
- ½ cup all-purpose flour
- ¼ cup cornmeal
- ½ teaspoon baking powder
- 1 large egg, beaten
- ¼ cup whole milk
- ¼ cup diced red bell pepper

Seasonings & Sauces:
- ½ teaspoon smoked paprika
- ½ teaspoon salt
- ¼ teaspoon black pepper
- ¼ teaspoon cayenne pepper

Optional Additions:
- 2 tablespoons chopped chives
- 2 tablespoons crumbled feta cheese

Nutritional Information
- **Calories:** 310 kcal
- **Carbs:** 40g
- **Fiber:** 5g
- **Protein:** 7g
- **Fats:** 12g
- **Sugar:** 3g

Instructions
1. **Preheat the Blackstone Griddle** to **medium heat** and lightly oil the surface.
2. Mix flour, cornmeal, baking powder, and seasonings in a bowl.
3. Stir in corn, red bell pepper, egg, and milk to form a batter.
4. Drop batter onto the griddle and cook **3–4 minutes per side** until golden brown.
5. Remove and serve hot with chives and feta.

Chef's Tips: Serve with honey butter or sour cream.
Notes: Use gluten-free flour for a gluten-free option.

All-American Cheeseburger Sliders

Prep Time: 10 minutes | **Cook Time:** 10 minutes | **Total Time:** 20 minutes

Ingredients
Main Ingredients:
- ½ pound ground beef (80/20 blend)
- 4 slider buns
- 2 slices American cheese, halved
- ¼ cup diced white onion

Seasonings & Sauces:
- ½ teaspoon salt
- ½ teaspoon black pepper
- ½ teaspoon garlic powder
- 1 tablespoon yellow mustard
- 1 tablespoon ketchup

Optional Additions:
- 4 pickle slices
- 1 tablespoon mayonnaise

Nutritional Information
- **Calories:** 450 kcal
- **Carbs:** 34g
- **Fiber:** 2g
- **Protein:** 22g
- **Fats:** 28g
- **Sugar:** 6g

Instructions
1. **Preheat the Blackstone Griddle** to **medium-high heat**.
2. Form ground beef into four thin patties and season both sides.
3. Cook patties **2–3 minutes per side**, adding onions before flipping.
4. Place cheese on patties and cover with a dome until melted.
5. Toast buns, assemble sliders with pickles, ketchup, and mustard.

Chef's Tips: Smash burgers onto the griddle for a crispier crust.
Notes: Use buttered buns for added richness.

1776 Philly Cheesesteak Bites

Prep Time: 10 minutes | **Cook Time:** 10 minutes | **Total Time:** 20 minutes

Ingredients
Main Ingredients:
- ½ pound thinly sliced ribeye steak
- 4 mini hoagie rolls
- ¼ cup sautéed onions
- ¼ cup sautéed bell peppers

Seasonings & Sauces:
- ½ teaspoon Worcestershire sauce
- ½ teaspoon salt
- ½ teaspoon black pepper
- ¼ teaspoon garlic powder
- ¼ cup melted provolone cheese

Optional Additions:
- 1 teaspoon hot sauce
- 1 teaspoon mayo

Nutritional Information
- **Calories:** 470 kcal
- **Carbs:** 42g
- **Fiber:** 3g
- **Protein:** 24g
- **Fats:** 22g
- **Sugar:** 4g

Instructions
1. **Preheat the Blackstone Griddle** to **medium-high heat**.
2. Cook onions and bell peppers for **3–4 minutes** until soft.
3. Add ribeye, season, and cook until browned.
4. Pile steak and veggies together, top with cheese, and cover with a dome.
5. Fill mini hoagie rolls and serve hot.

Chef's Tips: Freeze ribeye for 15 minutes for thinner slicing.
Notes: Use a griddle press for even cooking.

Frontier Campfire Queso Dip

Prep Time: 5 minutes | **Cook Time:** 10 minutes | **Total Time:** 15 minutes

Ingredients
Main Ingredients:
- 1 cup shredded cheddar cheese
- ½ cup shredded Monterey Jack cheese
- ¼ cup diced tomatoes with green chilies
- ¼ cup cooked chorizo

Seasonings & Sauces:
- ¼ teaspoon smoked paprika
- ¼ teaspoon cumin
- ¼ teaspoon garlic powder
- ¼ cup heavy cream

Optional Additions:
- 2 tablespoons chopped cilantro
- 1 teaspoon diced jalapeños

Nutritional Information
- **Calories:** 360 kcal
- **Carbs:** 8g
- **Fiber:** 1g
- **Protein:** 18g
- **Fats:** 28g
- **Sugar:** 3g

Instructions
1. **Preheat the Blackstone Griddle** to **low heat** and place a heatproof pan on top.
2. Add all ingredients, stirring occasionally until melted and smooth.
3. Simmer for **2–3 minutes**, then transfer to a serving dish.
4. Garnish with cilantro and serve with tortilla chips.

Chef's Tips: Use a melting dome for faster cheese melting.
Notes: Swap chorizo for sausage for a milder version.

BBQ Rodeo Onion Rings

Prep Time: 10 minutes | **Cook Time:** 10 minutes | **Total Time:** 20 minutes

Ingredients
Main Ingredients:
- 1 large sweet onion, sliced into thick rings
- ½ cup buttermilk
- ½ cup all-purpose flour
- ½ cup cornmeal
- 1 egg, beaten

Seasonings & Sauces:
- ½ teaspoon smoked paprika
- ½ teaspoon salt
- ¼ teaspoon black pepper
- ¼ teaspoon garlic powder
- ¼ cup BBQ sauce

Optional Additions:
- 2 tablespoons grated Parmesan
- 1 teaspoon cayenne for heat

Nutritional Information
- **Calories:** 320 kcal
- **Carbs:** 45g
- **Fiber:** 4g
- **Protein:** 6g
- **Fats:** 12g
- **Sugar:** 5g

Instructions
1. **Preheat the Blackstone Griddle** to **medium-high heat** and lightly oil the surface.
2. Dip onion rings in buttermilk, then dredge in a mixture of flour, cornmeal, and seasonings.
3. Coat in beaten egg, then dredge again in the dry mixture.
4. Place on the griddle and cook **3–4 minutes per side** until golden and crispy.
5. Remove, drizzle with BBQ sauce, and serve hot.

Chef's Tips: Use panko crumbs for extra crunch.
Notes: Adjust seasoning for a spicier or milder version.

Freedom Bacon-Wrapped Jalapeño Poppers

Prep Time: 10 minutes | **Cook Time:** 8 minutes | **Total Time:** 18 minutes

Ingredients
Main Ingredients:
- 4 large jalapeños, halved and deseeded
- 4 slices bacon, cut in half
- ½ cup cream cheese
- ¼ cup shredded cheddar cheese

Seasonings & Sauces:
- ½ teaspoon garlic powder
- ¼ teaspoon black pepper
- ¼ teaspoon smoked paprika

Optional Additions:
- 1 tablespoon finely chopped chives
- 1 teaspoon hot sauce

Nutritional Information
- **Calories:** 290 kcal
- **Carbs:** 5g
- **Fiber:** 1g
- **Protein:** 10g
- **Fats:** 26g
- **Sugar:** 2g

Instructions
1. **Preheat the Blackstone Griddle** to **medium heat**.
2. Mix cream cheese, cheddar, and seasonings in a bowl.
3. Fill each jalapeño half with cheese mixture and wrap with a half slice of bacon.
4. Place on the griddle, seam side down, and cook **3–4 minutes per side** until crispy.
5. Serve hot with optional chives or hot sauce.

Chef's Tips: Use toothpicks to secure bacon if needed.
Notes: Swap bacon for turkey bacon for a leaner version.

Buffalo Soldier Chicken Bites

Prep Time: 10 minutes | **Cook Time:** 12 minutes | **Total Time:** 22 minutes

Ingredients
Main Ingredients:
- ½ pound boneless, skinless chicken breast, cubed
- ¼ cup all-purpose flour
- ¼ cup cornstarch
- 1 egg, beaten

Seasonings & Sauces:
- ½ teaspoon salt
- ½ teaspoon black pepper
- ½ teaspoon garlic powder
- ¼ teaspoon cayenne pepper
- ¼ cup buffalo sauce

Optional Additions:
- 1 tablespoon melted butter
- 1 teaspoon honey for a sweeter glaze

Nutritional Information
- **Calories:** 350 kcal
- **Carbs:** 30g
- **Fiber:** 2g
- **Protein:** 28g
- **Fats:** 12g
- **Sugar:** 4g

Instructions
1. **Preheat the Blackstone Griddle** to **medium-high heat** and lightly oil the surface.
2. Coat chicken cubes in flour, cornstarch, and seasonings, then dip in beaten egg.
3. Place on the griddle and cook for **5–6 minutes per side** until golden brown.
4. Toss in buffalo sauce and serve hot.

Chef's Tips: Mix buffalo sauce with butter for a richer glaze.
Notes: Serve with ranch or blue cheese dressing.

Patriot Pretzel Bites with Beer Cheese

Prep Time: 15 minutes | **Cook Time:** 10 minutes | **Total Time:** 25 minutes

Ingredients
Main Ingredients:
- 1 cup premade pizza dough
- ¼ cup baking soda (for boiling water bath)
- 1 tablespoon coarse salt

Beer Cheese Sauce:
- ½ cup shredded sharp cheddar
- ¼ cup cream cheese
- ¼ cup beer (light lager or ale)
- ½ teaspoon garlic powder

Optional Additions:
- 1 teaspoon Dijon mustard in cheese sauce
- ¼ teaspoon cayenne for spice

Nutritional Information
- **Calories:** 410 kcal
- **Carbs:** 48g
- **Fiber:** 2g
- **Protein:** 12g
- **Fats:** 18g
- **Sugar:** 2g

Instructions
1. Roll pizza dough into a long rope and cut into bite-sized pieces.
2. Bring water to a boil and add baking soda, then briefly dip dough pieces in for **30 seconds**.
3. Transfer to the griddle and cook **3–4 minutes per side** until golden brown.
4. Melt cheese sauce ingredients together in a heatproof pan on the griddle.
5. Serve pretzel bites with warm beer cheese sauce.

Chef's Tips: Brush pretzels with butter for extra shine.
Notes: Swap beer for milk for an alcohol-free sauce.

Westward Ho' Grilled Cornbread Bites

P rep Time: 10 minutes | **Cook Time:** 12 minutes | **Total Time:** 22 minutes

Ingredients
Main Ingredients:
- ½ cup cornmeal
- ¼ cup all-purpose flour
- ½ teaspoon baking powder
- ¼ cup whole milk
- 1 egg, beaten

Seasonings & Sauces:
- ½ teaspoon salt
- ½ teaspoon sugar
- ¼ teaspoon black pepper
- 2 tablespoons melted butter

Optional Additions:
- ¼ cup shredded cheddar cheese
- 1 tablespoon honey

Nutritional Information
- **Calories:** 300 kcal
- **Carbs:** 38g
- **Fiber:** 4g
- **Protein:** 7g
- **Fats:** 12g
- **Sugar:** 6g

Instructions
1. **Preheat the Blackstone Griddle** to **medium heat**.
2. Mix all ingredients into a thick batter.
3. Spoon batter onto the griddle in small rounds and cook **4–5 minutes per side**.
4. Remove and serve with butter or honey.

Chef's Tips: Use buttermilk instead of milk for extra richness.
Notes: Add diced jalapeños for a spicy twist.

Smoky Uncle Sam Sausage Skewers

Prep Time: 10 minutes | **Cook Time:** 10 minutes | **Total Time:** 20 minutes

Ingredients
Main Ingredients:
- 2 smoked sausages, sliced into 1-inch rounds
- ½ red bell pepper, chopped into 1-inch pieces
- ½ green bell pepper, chopped into 1-inch pieces
- ½ red onion, chopped into 1-inch pieces
- 4 wooden skewers, soaked in water

Seasonings & Sauces:
- ½ teaspoon smoked paprika
- ½ teaspoon garlic powder
- ¼ teaspoon black pepper
- 1 tablespoon olive oil
- 2 tablespoons BBQ sauce

Optional Additions:
- 1 teaspoon hot sauce for extra heat
- ½ teaspoon honey for a touch of sweetness

Nutritional Information
- **Calories:** 380 kcal
- **Carbs:** 12g
- **Fiber:** 3g
- **Protein:** 18g
- **Fats:** 28g
- **Sugar:** 5g

Instructions
1. **Preheat the Blackstone Griddle** to **medium-high heat**.
2. Thread sausage slices, bell peppers, and onion onto skewers.
3. Brush skewers with olive oil and season with smoked paprika, garlic powder, and black pepper.
4. Cook for **4–5 minutes per side**, turning occasionally for even charring.
5. Brush with BBQ sauce in the final minute, then remove and serve hot.

Chef's Tips: Rotate skewers frequently for even grilling.
Notes: Use metal skewers for a reusable option.

Red, White & Blueberry Griddle Pancake Stacks

P rep Time: 10 minutes | **Cook Time:** 8 minutes | **Total Time:** 18 minutes

Ingredients
Main Ingredients:
- 1 cup pancake mix
- ¾ cup whole milk
- 1 egg
- ½ teaspoon vanilla extract
- ¼ cup blueberries
- ¼ cup diced strawberries

Seasonings & Sauces:
- 1 teaspoon granulated sugar
- ¼ teaspoon cinnamon
- 1 tablespoon melted butter
- 2 tablespoons maple syrup

Optional Additions:
- 1 tablespoon whipped cream
- 1 teaspoon lemon zest

Nutritional Information
- **Calories:** 310 kcal
- **Carbs:** 45g
- **Fiber:** 3g
- **Protein:** 8g
- **Fats:** 10g
- **Sugar:** 15g

Instructions
1. **Preheat the Blackstone Griddle** to **medium-low heat** and lightly grease the surface.
2. Mix pancake batter, sugar, cinnamon, and vanilla in a bowl.
3. Pour small rounds of batter onto the griddle, then top each with blueberries and strawberries.
4. Cook for **2–3 minutes per side**, flipping once bubbles form.
5. Stack pancakes and drizzle with maple syrup.

Chef's Tips: Keep pancakes warm by tenting with foil.
Notes: Swap regular milk with almond milk for a dairy-free version.

Great Plains Griddled Cheese Curds

Prep Time: 5 minutes | **Cook Time:** 7 minutes | **Total Time:** 12 minutes

Ingredients
Main Ingredients:
- 1 cup cheese curds
- ½ cup all-purpose flour
- 1 egg, beaten
- ½ cup panko breadcrumbs

Seasonings & Sauces:
- ½ teaspoon salt
- ½ teaspoon black pepper
- ¼ teaspoon garlic powder
- ¼ teaspoon smoked paprika

Optional Additions:
- 1 tablespoon chopped parsley for garnish
- ¼ cup ranch or marinara for dipping

Nutritional Information
- **Calories:** 350 kcal
- **Carbs:** 30g
- **Fiber:** 2g
- **Protein:** 15g
- **Fats:** 20g
- **Sugar:** 1g

Instructions
1. **Preheat the Blackstone Griddle** to **medium heat** and lightly oil the surface.
2. Coat cheese curds in flour, then dip in egg and coat with panko breadcrumbs.
3. Place on the griddle and cook **2–3 minutes per side** until golden brown.
4. Remove from heat and serve with dipping sauce.

Chef's Tips: Freeze cheese curds for 15 minutes before frying to prevent melting.
Notes: Use gluten-free panko for a GF-friendly option.

Southern Glory Fried Pickle Chips

Prep Time: 10 minutes | **Cook Time:** 8 minutes | **Total Time:** 18 minutes

Ingredients
Main Ingredients:
- ½ cup sliced dill pickles
- ½ cup all-purpose flour
- ¼ cup cornmeal
- 1 egg, beaten

Seasonings & Sauces:
- ½ teaspoon salt
- ¼ teaspoon black pepper
- ¼ teaspoon cayenne pepper
- ½ teaspoon garlic powder

Optional Additions:
- ¼ cup ranch dressing for dipping
- 1 tablespoon hot sauce for extra heat

Nutritional Information
- **Calories:** 280 kcal
- **Carbs:** 35g
- **Fiber:** 3g
- **Protein:** 6g
- **Fats:** 12g
- **Sugar:** 2g

Instructions
1. **Preheat the Blackstone Griddle** to **medium heat**.
2. Coat pickle slices in flour, then dip in egg and dredge in cornmeal mixture.
3. Cook on the griddle for **3–4 minutes per side** until golden and crispy.
4. Remove and serve with ranch dressing.

Chef's Tips: Pat pickles dry before coating for extra crunch.
Notes: Use gluten-free flour for a GF-friendly version.

The Founding Fathers' Fried Mac & Cheese Bites

Prep Time: 15 minutes | **Cook Time:** 10 minutes | **Total Time:** 25 minutes

Ingredients
Main Ingredients:
- 1 cup cooked mac & cheese, chilled
- ½ cup all-purpose flour
- 1 egg, beaten
- ½ cup panko breadcrumbs

Seasonings & Sauces:
- ½ teaspoon salt
- ¼ teaspoon black pepper
- ¼ teaspoon smoked paprika
- ¼ teaspoon garlic powder

Optional Additions:
- ¼ cup marinara or ranch for dipping
- 1 teaspoon hot sauce for extra spice

Nutritional Information
- **Calories:** 400 kcal
- **Carbs:** 45g
- **Fiber:** 2g
- **Protein:** 12g
- **Fats:** 18g
- **Sugar:** 3g

Instructions
1. **Preheat the Blackstone Griddle** to **medium heat**.
2. Shape chilled mac & cheese into small balls and freeze for 10 minutes.
3. Coat in flour, dip in egg, then cover with panko breadcrumbs.
4. Place on the griddle and cook **3–4 minutes per side** until crispy.
5. Remove and serve with dipping sauce.

Chef's Tips: Let mac & cheese chill completely before forming balls.
Notes: Swap cheddar for pepper jack for extra heat.

CHAPTER 4: FLAVORFUL VEGETABLES & SIDE DISHES

Liberty Skillet Corn with Honey Butter

Prep Time: 5 minutes | **Cook Time:** 10 minutes | **Total Time:** 15 minutes

Ingredients
Main Ingredients:
- 2 ears fresh corn, kernels removed
- 1 tablespoon unsalted butter
- 1 teaspoon olive oil

Seasonings & Sauces:
- ½ teaspoon smoked paprika
- ½ teaspoon salt
- ¼ teaspoon black pepper
- 1 teaspoon honey

Optional Additions:
- 1 tablespoon chopped fresh parsley
- ¼ teaspoon cayenne pepper for heat

Nutritional Information
- **Calories:** 180 kcal
- **Carbs:** 26g
- **Fiber:** 3g
- **Protein:** 3g
- **Fats:** 8g
- **Sugar:** 8g

Instructions
1. **Preheat the Blackstone Griddle** to **medium heat** and add butter and olive oil.
2. Spread corn evenly on the griddle and cook **6–8 minutes**, stirring occasionally.
3. Sprinkle with paprika, salt, and pepper, then drizzle with honey.
4. Cook for **1–2 minutes**, stirring until caramelized.
5. Remove and garnish with parsley if desired.

Chef's Tips: Use frozen corn if fresh isn't available.
Notes: Add cayenne for a spicy-sweet balance.

Stars & Stripes Sweet Potato Hash

Prep Time: 10 minutes | **Cook Time:** 12 minutes | **Total Time:** 22 minutes

Ingredients
Main Ingredients:
- 1 medium sweet potato, peeled and diced
- ½ small red bell pepper, diced
- ½ small green bell pepper, diced
- ½ small onion, chopped

Seasonings & Sauces:
- ½ teaspoon salt
- ½ teaspoon garlic powder
- ¼ teaspoon cinnamon
- ¼ teaspoon black pepper
- 1 tablespoon olive oil

Optional Additions:
- ¼ teaspoon red pepper flakes for heat
- 1 tablespoon chopped fresh cilantro

Nutritional Information
- **Calories:** 220 kcal
- **Carbs:** 40g
- **Fiber:** 5g
- **Protein:** 3g
- **Fats:** 6g
- **Sugar:** 9g

Instructions
1. **Preheat the Blackstone Griddle** to **medium heat** and drizzle with olive oil.
2. Add diced sweet potatoes, spreading them in a single layer. Cook **5 minutes**, stirring occasionally.
3. Add bell peppers and onion, seasoning with salt, garlic powder, cinnamon, and pepper.
4. Cook for **6–7 minutes** until potatoes are tender and slightly crispy.
5. Remove and sprinkle with red pepper flakes or cilantro if desired.

Chef's Tips: Cook in batches to avoid overcrowding the griddle.
Notes: Swap cinnamon for smoked paprika for a savory version.

Frontier-Style Griddled Green Beans with Bacon

Prep Time: 5 minutes | **Cook Time:** 8 minutes | **Total Time:** 13 minutes

Ingredients
Main Ingredients:
- 2 cups fresh green beans, trimmed
- 2 slices thick-cut bacon, chopped
- ½ small shallot, finely diced

Seasonings & Sauces:
- ½ teaspoon salt
- ¼ teaspoon black pepper
- ½ teaspoon smoked paprika
- 1 teaspoon apple cider vinegar

Optional Additions:
- 1 tablespoon slivered almonds
- ½ teaspoon crushed red pepper

Nutritional Information
- **Calories:** 250 kcal
- **Carbs:** 15g
- **Fiber:** 5g
- **Protein:** 8g
- **Fats:** 18g
- **Sugar:** 4g

Instructions
1. **Preheat the Blackstone Griddle** to **medium heat** and cook bacon until crispy.
2. Add shallots and cook for **1 minute**, stirring to coat in bacon fat.
3. Toss in green beans and season with salt, pepper, and smoked paprika.
4. Cook for **5–6 minutes**, stirring occasionally, until beans are slightly charred.
5. Drizzle with apple cider vinegar before serving.

Chef's Tips: Use thinner green beans for quicker cooking.
Notes: Add slivered almonds for extra crunch.

The Founding Farmers' Homestyle Smashed Potatoes

Prep Time: 10 minutes | **Cook Time:** 15 minutes | **Total Time:** 25 minutes

Ingredients
Main Ingredients:
- 4 small Yukon Gold potatoes, boiled until fork-tender
- 1 tablespoon unsalted butter
- 1 tablespoon olive oil

Seasonings & Sauces:
- ½ teaspoon salt
- ¼ teaspoon black pepper
- ½ teaspoon garlic powder
- ½ teaspoon fresh rosemary, chopped

Optional Additions:
- 1 tablespoon grated Parmesan
- ½ teaspoon smoked paprika

Nutritional Information
- **Calories:** 280 kcal
- **Carbs:** 35g
- **Fiber:** 4g
- **Protein:** 4g
- **Fats:** 14g
- **Sugar:** 2g

Instructions
1. **Preheat the Blackstone Griddle** to **medium-high heat** and melt butter with olive oil.
2. Place boiled potatoes on the griddle and smash them flat with a spatula.
3. Season with salt, pepper, garlic powder, and rosemary.
4. Cook for **5–6 minutes per side** until crispy and golden brown.
5. Remove and sprinkle with Parmesan or smoked paprika.

Chef's Tips: Press potatoes firmly for crispier edges.
Notes: Swap Yukon Gold for red potatoes for a different texture.

Smoky Appalachian Grilled Brussels Sprouts

Prep Time: 5 minutes | **Cook Time:** 10 minutes | **Total Time:** 15 minutes

Ingredients
Main Ingredients:
- 2 cups Brussels sprouts, halved
- 1 tablespoon olive oil
- ½ small red onion, sliced

Seasonings & Sauces:
- ½ teaspoon salt
- ¼ teaspoon black pepper
- ½ teaspoon smoked paprika
- 1 teaspoon balsamic glaze

Optional Additions:
- 1 tablespoon chopped pecans
- 1 teaspoon honey for sweetness

Nutritional Information
- **Calories:** 200 kcal
- **Carbs:** 18g
- **Fiber:** 6g
- **Protein:** 5g
- **Fats:** 10g
- **Sugar:** 7g

Instructions
1. **Preheat the Blackstone Griddle** to **medium heat** and drizzle with olive oil.
2. Spread Brussels sprouts cut-side down and add sliced red onion.
3. Cook for **7–8 minutes**, stirring occasionally, until slightly charred.
4. Season with salt, black pepper, and smoked paprika.
5. Drizzle with balsamic glaze before serving.

Chef's Tips: Cut sprouts evenly for uniform cooking.
Notes: Add pecans for crunch or honey for a sweet-savory balance.

American Dream Cheesy Hash Browns

Prep Time: 5 minutes | **Cook Time:** 12 minutes | **Total Time:** 17 minutes

Ingredients
Main Ingredients:
- 2 cups shredded russet potatoes, rinsed and dried
- ½ cup shredded sharp cheddar cheese
- 1 tablespoon unsalted butter
- 1 tablespoon olive oil

Seasonings & Sauces:
- ½ teaspoon salt
- ¼ teaspoon black pepper
- ¼ teaspoon smoked paprika
- ¼ teaspoon garlic powder

Optional Additions:
- 1 tablespoon chopped chives
- 1 tablespoon sour cream for topping

Nutritional Information
- **Calories:** 310 kcal
- **Carbs:** 35g
- **Fiber:** 3g
- **Protein:** 8g
- **Fats:** 16g
- **Sugar:** 2g

Instructions
1. **Preheat the Blackstone Griddle** to **medium heat** and melt butter with olive oil.
2. Spread shredded potatoes evenly on the griddle and press down with a spatula.
3. Cook for **5–6 minutes** until golden brown, then flip and cook another **5 minutes**.
4. Sprinkle with cheddar cheese, cover with a dome, and let melt for **1 minute**.
5. Remove from the griddle and garnish with chives and sour cream if desired.

Chef's Tips: Rinse shredded potatoes in cold water and pat dry for extra crispiness.
Notes: Swap cheddar for pepper jack for a spicier twist.

Westward Ho' Cowboy Baked Beans

Prep Time: 5 minutes | **Cook Time:** 15 minutes | **Total Time:** 20 minutes

Ingredients
Main Ingredients:
- 1 cup canned baked beans
- ¼ cup diced smoked sausage
- ¼ cup diced onions
- ¼ cup diced red bell pepper

Seasonings & Sauces:
- ½ teaspoon smoked paprika
- ½ teaspoon Worcestershire sauce
- ¼ teaspoon salt
- ¼ teaspoon black pepper

Optional Additions:
- 1 teaspoon hot sauce for heat
- 1 tablespoon brown sugar for sweetness

Nutritional Information
- **Calories:** 280 kcal
- **Carbs:** 35g
- **Fiber:** 8g
- **Protein:** 12g
- **Fats:** 10g
- **Sugar:** 12g

Instructions
1. **Preheat the Blackstone Griddle** to **medium-low heat** and lightly oil the surface.
2. Cook diced sausage, onions, and bell peppers for **4–5 minutes** until softened.
3. Add baked beans, smoked paprika, Worcestershire sauce, salt, and pepper.
4. Stir and let simmer for **6–7 minutes** until thickened.
5. Serve hot with additional hot sauce if desired.

Chef's Tips: Let beans cook longer for a richer flavor.
Notes: Use turkey sausage for a leaner version.

Griddle-Seared Maple Glazed Carrots

Prep Time: 5 minutes | **Cook Time:** 10 minutes | **Total Time:** 15 minutes

Ingredients
Main Ingredients:
- 2 cups baby carrots, halved
- 1 tablespoon unsalted butter
- 1 tablespoon olive oil

Seasonings & Sauces:
- 1 tablespoon maple syrup
- ½ teaspoon salt
- ¼ teaspoon black pepper
- ¼ teaspoon cinnamon

Optional Additions:
- 1 tablespoon chopped pecans
- ½ teaspoon red pepper flakes for heat

Nutritional Information
- **Calories:** 190 kcal
- **Carbs:** 26g
- **Fiber:** 5g
- **Protein:** 2g
- **Fats:** 10g
- **Sugar:** 14g

Instructions
1. **Preheat the Blackstone Griddle** to **medium heat** and melt butter with olive oil.
2. Spread carrots on the griddle and cook for **5–6 minutes**, stirring occasionally.
3. Drizzle with maple syrup, then season with salt, black pepper, and cinnamon.
4. Cook for **2–3 more minutes** until caramelized.
5. Remove and garnish with pecans or red pepper flakes if desired.

Chef's Tips: Slice carrots evenly for uniform cooking.
Notes: Swap maple syrup for honey for a different sweetness.

Great Plains Garlic Butter Mushrooms

Prep Time: 5 minutes | **Cook Time:** 8 minutes | **Total Time:** 13 minutes

Ingredients
Main Ingredients:
- 2 cups cremini mushrooms, halved
- 1 tablespoon unsalted butter
- 1 tablespoon olive oil
- 1 clove garlic, minced

Seasonings & Sauces:
- ½ teaspoon salt
- ¼ teaspoon black pepper
- ½ teaspoon fresh thyme

Optional Additions:
- 1 teaspoon balsamic glaze
- 1 tablespoon grated Parmesan

Nutritional Information
- **Calories:** 170 kcal
- **Carbs:** 10g
- **Fiber:** 2g
- **Protein:** 4g
- **Fats:** 14g
- **Sugar:** 3g

Instructions
1. **Preheat the Blackstone Griddle** to **medium heat** and add butter and olive oil.
2. Add mushrooms and cook for **4–5 minutes**, stirring occasionally.
3. Stir in garlic, salt, black pepper, and thyme, cooking for **2 more minutes**.
4. Remove from heat and drizzle with balsamic glaze or sprinkle with Parmesan.

Chef's Tips: Avoid overcrowding to allow mushrooms to brown properly.
Notes: Swap cremini mushrooms for white button mushrooms if preferred.

1776 Loaded Griddle Fries

Prep Time: 10 minutes | **Cook Time:** 12 minutes | **Total Time:** 22 minutes

Ingredients
Main Ingredients:
- 2 medium russet potatoes, cut into thin fries
- ½ cup shredded cheddar cheese
- 2 slices bacon, cooked and crumbled

Seasonings & Sauces:
- ½ teaspoon salt
- ¼ teaspoon black pepper
- ¼ teaspoon garlic powder
- ½ teaspoon smoked paprika

Optional Additions:
- 1 tablespoon sour cream for topping
- 1 tablespoon diced green onions

Nutritional Information
- **Calories:** 380 kcal
- **Carbs:** 50g
- **Fiber:** 5g
- **Protein:** 12g
- **Fats:** 16g
- **Sugar:** 3g

Instructions
1. **Preheat the Blackstone Griddle** to **medium-high heat** and drizzle with oil.
2. Spread potato fries in an even layer and season with salt, pepper, garlic powder, and paprika.
3. Cook for **8–10 minutes**, flipping occasionally until crispy.
4. Sprinkle with shredded cheese and crumbled bacon, then cover with a dome to melt cheese.
5. Remove and top with sour cream and green onions if desired.

Chef's Tips: Soak potato fries in cold water for 20 minutes before cooking for extra crispiness.

Notes: Swap cheddar for Monterey Jack for a different flavor.

Southern Glory Collard Greens & Cornbread Crumbles

Prep Time: 10 minutes | **Cook Time:** 15 minutes | **Total Time:** 25 minutes

Ingredients
Main Ingredients:
- 2 cups chopped fresh collard greens
- ¼ cup diced smoked bacon
- ½ cup crumbled cornbread
- ½ small onion, diced

Seasonings & Sauces:
- ½ teaspoon salt
- ¼ teaspoon black pepper
- ½ teaspoon garlic powder
- 1 teaspoon apple cider vinegar
- ½ teaspoon red pepper flakes

Optional Additions:
- 1 teaspoon honey for a touch of sweetness
- 1 tablespoon chopped scallions

Nutritional Information
- **Calories:** 320 kcal
- **Carbs:** 40g
- **Fiber:** 6g
- **Protein:** 10g
- **Fats:** 14g
- **Sugar:** 6g

Instructions
1. **Preheat the Blackstone Griddle** to **medium heat** and cook bacon until crispy.
2. Add onions and collard greens, cooking for **6–7 minutes** until softened.
3. Season with salt, pepper, garlic powder, and red pepper flakes.
4. Stir in apple cider vinegar and cook for **2 more minutes**.
5. Remove from heat and top with cornbread crumbles.

Chef's Tips: Use pre-washed, chopped greens for convenience.
Notes: Swap bacon for smoked turkey for a lighter version.

Crispy Uncle Sam's Zucchini Fritters

Prep Time: 10 minutes | **Cook Time:** 10 minutes | **Total Time:** 20 minutes

Ingredients
Main Ingredients:
- 1 medium zucchini, grated and squeezed dry
- ¼ cup all-purpose flour
- ¼ cup grated Parmesan cheese
- 1 egg, beaten

Seasonings & Sauces:
- ½ teaspoon salt
- ¼ teaspoon black pepper
- ¼ teaspoon garlic powder
- ½ teaspoon dried oregano

Optional Additions:
- 1 teaspoon lemon zest for brightness
- ¼ cup sour cream for dipping

Nutritional Information
- **Calories:** 250 kcal
- **Carbs:** 28g
- **Fiber:** 4g
- **Protein:** 9g
- **Fats:** 12g
- **Sugar:** 3g

Instructions
1. **Preheat the Blackstone Griddle** to **medium heat** and lightly oil the surface.
2. Mix zucchini, flour, Parmesan, egg, and seasonings in a bowl.
3. Scoop small portions onto the griddle and flatten slightly.
4. Cook for **4–5 minutes per side** until crispy and golden brown.
5. Remove and serve with sour cream.

Chef's Tips: Squeeze zucchini well to remove excess moisture.
Notes: Add shredded carrots for extra texture.

Red, White & Blueberry Summer Slaw

Prep Time: 10 minutes | **Cook Time:** 0 minutes | **Total Time:** 10 minutes

Ingredients
Main Ingredients:
- 1 cup shredded green cabbage
- ½ cup shredded red cabbage
- ¼ cup julienned carrots
- ¼ cup fresh blueberries

Seasonings & Sauces:
- ¼ cup Greek yogurt or mayo
- 1 tablespoon apple cider vinegar
- 1 teaspoon honey
- ½ teaspoon salt
- ¼ teaspoon black pepper

Optional Additions:
- 1 tablespoon chopped pecans
- 1 teaspoon poppy seeds

Nutritional Information
- **Calories:** 180 kcal
- **Carbs:** 25g
- **Fiber:** 6g
- **Protein:** 4g
- **Fats:** 6g
- **Sugar:** 12g

Instructions
1. In a bowl, mix cabbage, carrots, and blueberries.
2. In a separate bowl, whisk together yogurt, vinegar, honey, salt, and pepper.
3. Pour dressing over the slaw and toss until well combined.
4. Let sit for **5 minutes** before serving.

Chef's Tips: Use red apples instead of blueberries for a crunchy twist.
Notes: Refrigerate for an hour for deeper flavor.

Patriot-Style Fire-Roasted Peppers & Onions

Prep Time: 5 minutes | **Cook Time:** 10 minutes | **Total Time:** 15 minutes

Ingredients
Main Ingredients:
- ½ red bell pepper, sliced
- ½ green bell pepper, sliced
- ½ small red onion, sliced

Seasonings & Sauces:
- ½ teaspoon salt
- ¼ teaspoon black pepper
- ½ teaspoon smoked paprika
- 1 tablespoon olive oil

Optional Additions:
- 1 teaspoon balsamic vinegar for added depth
- ¼ teaspoon chili flakes for heat

Nutritional Information
- **Calories:** 140 kcal
- **Carbs:** 18g
- **Fiber:** 5g
- **Protein:** 2g
- **Fats:** 7g
- **Sugar:** 9g

Instructions
1. **Preheat the Blackstone Griddle** to **medium-high heat** and drizzle with oil.
2. Add peppers and onions, spreading them in a single layer.
3. Season with salt, black pepper, and smoked paprika.
4. Cook for **6–8 minutes**, stirring occasionally, until softened and slightly charred.
5. Remove and drizzle with balsamic vinegar if desired.

Chef's Tips: Use multicolored bell peppers for a vibrant dish.
Notes: Serve as a side or use as a topping for tacos.

All-American Griddled Mac & Cheese

Prep Time: 10 minutes | **Cook Time:** 12 minutes | **Total Time:** 22 minutes

Ingredients
Main Ingredients:
- 1 cup cooked mac & cheese, chilled
- ¼ cup shredded sharp cheddar
- ¼ cup panko breadcrumbs
- 1 tablespoon unsalted butter

Seasonings & Sauces:
- ½ teaspoon salt
- ¼ teaspoon black pepper
- ¼ teaspoon garlic powder

Optional Additions:
- 1 teaspoon Dijon mustard for tang
- 1 tablespoon chopped crispy bacon

Nutritional Information
- **Calories:** 420 kcal
- **Carbs:** 45g
- **Fiber:** 3g
- **Protein:** 12g
- **Fats:** 18g
- **Sugar:** 4g

Instructions
1. **Preheat the Blackstone Griddle** to **medium heat** and melt butter.
2. Form chilled mac & cheese into small patties.
3. Coat in panko breadcrumbs and place on the griddle.
4. Cook for **5–6 minutes per side** until golden brown.
5. Remove and serve with crispy bacon or mustard if desired.

Chef's Tips: Let mac & cheese chill overnight for better shaping.
Notes: Use gluten-free breadcrumbs for a GF version.

CHAPTER 5: EASY MEAT RECIPES

Liberty Bell Griddle-Seared Ribeye

Prep Time: 5 minutes | **Cook Time:** 10 minutes | **Total Time:** 15 minutes

Ingredients
Main Ingredients:
- 1 (12 oz) ribeye steak, about 1-inch thick
- 1 tablespoon unsalted butter
- 1 teaspoon olive oil

Seasonings & Sauces:
- ½ teaspoon kosher salt
- ½ teaspoon black pepper
- ½ teaspoon garlic powder
- ¼ teaspoon smoked paprika

Optional Additions:
- 1 teaspoon fresh rosemary, chopped
- ½ teaspoon crushed red pepper for heat

Nutritional Information
- **Calories:** 650 kcal
- **Carbs:** 2g
- **Fiber:** 0g
- **Protein:** 50g
- **Fats:** 48g
- **Sugar:** 0g

Instructions
1. **Preheat the Blackstone Griddle** to **high heat** and drizzle with olive oil.
2. Season the ribeye with salt, black pepper, garlic powder, and smoked paprika.
3. Place the steak on the griddle and sear for **4–5 minutes per side**, flipping only once.
4. In the last minute of cooking, add butter and rosemary, basting the steak.
5. Remove from heat and let rest for **5 minutes** before slicing.

Chef's Tips: Let steak come to room temperature before cooking for even searing.
Notes: Use a meat thermometer to reach 130°F for medium-rare.

1776 Maple-Glazed Pork Chops

Prep Time: 10 minutes | **Cook Time:** 12 minutes | **Total Time:** 22 minutes

Ingredients
Main Ingredients:
- 2 (6 oz) bone-in pork chops
- 1 tablespoon olive oil
- 1 tablespoon unsalted butter

Seasonings & Sauces:
- ½ teaspoon kosher salt
- ¼ teaspoon black pepper
- ½ teaspoon garlic powder
- 2 tablespoons maple syrup
- 1 teaspoon Dijon mustard

Optional Additions:
- ½ teaspoon apple cider vinegar for tang
- ½ teaspoon crushed red pepper for spice

Nutritional Information
- **Calories:** 420 kcal
- **Carbs:** 10g
- **Fiber:** 0g
- **Protein:** 35g
- **Fats:** 28g
- **Sugar:** 8g

Instructions
1. **Preheat the Blackstone Griddle** to **medium heat** and drizzle with olive oil.
2. Season pork chops with salt, pepper, and garlic powder.
3. Sear for **5–6 minutes per side**, flipping once.
4. In the last 2 minutes, brush with a glaze of maple syrup and Dijon mustard.
5. Remove from heat and let rest for **3 minutes** before serving.

Chef's Tips: Baste with extra glaze in the last minute for more flavor.
Notes: Use thick-cut chops to prevent overcooking.

Frontier-Style Cowboy Steak Bites

Prep Time: 5 minutes | **Cook Time:** 8 minutes | **Total Time:** 13 minutes

Ingredients
Main Ingredients:
- 8 oz sirloin steak, cut into bite-sized cubes
- 1 tablespoon olive oil
- 1 tablespoon unsalted butter

Seasonings & Sauces:
- ½ teaspoon kosher salt
- ¼ teaspoon black pepper
- ½ teaspoon smoked paprika
- ½ teaspoon garlic powder

Optional Additions:
- 1 teaspoon Worcestershire sauce
- ½ teaspoon crushed red pepper for heat

Nutritional Information
- **Calories:** 450 kcal
- **Carbs:** 2g
- **Fiber:** 0g
- **Protein:** 38g
- **Fats:** 30g
- **Sugar:** 0g

Instructions
1. **Preheat the Blackstone Griddle** to **medium-high heat** and drizzle with oil.
2. Toss steak cubes with salt, black pepper, smoked paprika, and garlic powder.
3. Cook steak bites for **3–4 minutes per side**, stirring occasionally.
4. In the last minute, add butter and Worcestershire sauce, tossing to coat.
5. Remove from heat and serve hot.

Chef's Tips: Let steak bites develop a crust before stirring.
Notes: Use ribeye for extra tenderness.

Stars & Stripes Honey BBQ Chicken Thighs

Prep Time: 10 minutes | **Cook Time:** 14 minutes | **Total Time:** 24 minutes

Ingredients
Main Ingredients:
- 2 boneless, skinless chicken thighs
- 1 tablespoon olive oil
- 1 tablespoon unsalted butter

Seasonings & Sauces:
- ½ teaspoon salt
- ¼ teaspoon black pepper
- ½ teaspoon smoked paprika
- 2 tablespoons BBQ sauce
- 1 teaspoon honey

Optional Additions:
- ½ teaspoon mustard for tang
- ½ teaspoon chili powder for spice

Nutritional Information
- **Calories:** 380 kcal
- **Carbs:** 12g
- **Fiber:** 0g
- **Protein:** 35g
- **Fats:** 22g
- **Sugar:** 10g

Instructions
1. **Preheat the Blackstone Griddle** to **medium heat** and drizzle with oil.
2. Season chicken thighs with salt, pepper, paprika, and garlic powder.
3. Cook for **6–7 minutes per side**, flipping once.
4. In the last minute, brush with a mix of BBQ sauce and honey.
5. Remove from heat and let rest for **3 minutes** before serving.

Chef's Tips: Use bone-in thighs for juicier results.
Notes: Swap BBQ sauce for teriyaki for a different twist.

All-American Griddled Meatloaf Patties

Prep Time: 10 minutes | **Cook Time:** 10 minutes | **Total Time:** 20 minutes

Ingredients
Main Ingredients:
- ½ pound ground beef (80/20)
- ¼ cup breadcrumbs
- 1 egg, beaten
- 2 tablespoons ketchup

Seasonings & Sauces:
- ½ teaspoon salt
- ¼ teaspoon black pepper
- ½ teaspoon garlic powder
- ½ teaspoon onion powder

Optional Additions:
- ½ teaspoon Worcestershire sauce
- 1 tablespoon chopped parsley

Nutritional Information
- **Calories:** 420 kcal
- **Carbs:** 15g
- **Fiber:** 1g
- **Protein:** 28g
- **Fats:** 28g
- **Sugar:** 4g

Instructions
1. **Preheat the Blackstone Griddle** to **medium heat** and lightly oil the surface.
2. Mix ground beef, breadcrumbs, egg, ketchup, and seasonings in a bowl.
3. Shape into two patties and cook for **4–5 minutes per side**.
4. Remove from heat and let rest for **2 minutes** before serving.

Chef's Tips: Press patties slightly in the center to prevent bulging.
Notes: Serve with mashed potatoes for a classic pairing.

Buffalo Soldier Spicy Chicken Tenders

Prep Time: 10 minutes | **Cook Time:** 10 minutes | **Total Time:** 20 minutes

Ingredients
Main Ingredients:
- 2 boneless, skinless chicken breasts, cut into strips
- ½ cup buttermilk
- ½ cup all-purpose flour
- ¼ cup cornstarch

Seasonings & Sauces:
- ½ teaspoon salt
- ½ teaspoon black pepper
- ½ teaspoon smoked paprika
- ½ teaspoon garlic powder
- ¼ teaspoon cayenne pepper
- ¼ cup buffalo sauce

Optional Additions:
- 1 tablespoon melted butter for sauce
- 1 teaspoon honey for a touch of sweetness

Nutritional Information
- **Calories:** 420 kcal
- **Carbs:** 38g
- **Fiber:** 2g
- **Protein:** 34g
- **Fats:** 14g
- **Sugar:** 4g

Instructions
1. **Preheat the Blackstone Griddle** to **medium-high heat** and lightly oil the surface.
2. Soak chicken strips in buttermilk for **5 minutes**, then coat in flour, cornstarch, and seasonings.
3. Cook for **4–5 minutes per side**, flipping once, until golden brown.
4. Toss in buffalo sauce before serving.

Chef's Tips: Let coated chicken rest for 5 minutes before cooking for a crispier crust.
Notes: Serve with ranch or blue cheese dressing.

Uncle Sam's Smoked Sausage & Peppers

Prep Time: 5 minutes | **Cook Time:** 10 minutes | **Total Time:** 15 minutes

Ingredients
Main Ingredients:
- 2 smoked sausages, sliced
- ½ red bell pepper, sliced
- ½ green bell pepper, sliced
- ½ red onion, sliced

Seasonings & Sauces:
- ½ teaspoon salt
- ¼ teaspoon black pepper
- ½ teaspoon garlic powder
- ½ teaspoon Italian seasoning

Optional Additions:
- 1 teaspoon balsamic vinegar for extra depth
- ¼ teaspoon red pepper flakes for spice

Nutritional Information
- **Calories:** 380 kcal
- **Carbs:** 12g
- **Fiber:** 3g
- **Protein:** 18g
- **Fats:** 28g
- **Sugar:** 4g

Instructions
1. **Preheat the Blackstone Griddle** to **medium heat** and drizzle with oil.
2. Cook sausage slices for **3–4 minutes**, stirring occasionally.
3. Add peppers and onions, seasoning with salt, black pepper, garlic powder, and Italian seasoning.
4. Cook for **5–6 minutes**, stirring occasionally, until vegetables are softened.

Chef's Tips: Use spicy sausage for extra heat.
Notes: Serve over rice or in a hoagie roll.

Southern Glory Country-Fried Steak

Prep Time: 10 minutes | **Cook Time:** 12 minutes | **Total Time:** 22 minutes

Ingredients
Main Ingredients:
- 2 cube steaks
- ½ cup all-purpose flour
- ½ cup buttermilk
- 1 egg, beaten

Seasonings & Sauces:
- ½ teaspoon salt
- ½ teaspoon black pepper
- ½ teaspoon smoked paprika
- ½ teaspoon garlic powder

Optional Additions:
- ½ teaspoon cayenne for spice
- ¼ cup country gravy for topping

Nutritional Information
- **Calories:** 450 kcal
- **Carbs:** 35g
- **Fiber:** 2g
- **Protein:** 36g
- **Fats:** 20g
- **Sugar:** 3g

Instructions
1. **Preheat the Blackstone Griddle** to **medium heat** and lightly oil the surface.
2. Dredge cube steaks in flour, dip in buttermilk and egg, then coat in flour again.
3. Cook for **5–6 minutes per side**, flipping once, until crispy and golden brown.
4. Remove from heat and serve with country gravy.

Chef's Tips: Let breaded steaks rest for 5 minutes before cooking to help the coating stick.

Notes: Use gluten-free flour for a GF version.

Westward Ho' Garlic Butter Pork Medallions

Prep Time: 5 minutes | **Cook Time:** 10 minutes | **Total Time:** 15 minutes

Ingredients
Main Ingredients:
- 8 oz pork tenderloin, cut into medallions
- 1 tablespoon unsalted butter
- 1 teaspoon olive oil

Seasonings & Sauces:
- ½ teaspoon salt
- ¼ teaspoon black pepper
- ½ teaspoon garlic powder
- ½ teaspoon dried thyme

Optional Additions:
- 1 teaspoon Dijon mustard for tang
- ½ teaspoon lemon juice for brightness

Nutritional Information
- **Calories:** 320 kcal
- **Carbs:** 2g
- **Fiber:** 0g
- **Protein:** 42g
- **Fats:** 16g
- **Sugar:** 0g

Instructions
1. **Preheat the Blackstone Griddle** to **medium-high heat** and drizzle with olive oil.
2. Season pork medallions with salt, black pepper, garlic powder, and thyme.
3. Cook for **4–5 minutes per side**, flipping once.
4. In the last minute, add butter and baste the pork.

Chef's Tips: Let pork rest for 5 minutes before slicing for juicier meat.
Notes: Swap thyme for rosemary for a different flavor.

Great Plains Griddled Turkey Cutlets with Herb Butter

Prep Time: 5 minutes | **Cook Time:** 8 minutes | **Total Time:** 13 minutes

Ingredients
Main Ingredients:
- 2 turkey cutlets (4 oz each)
- 1 tablespoon olive oil
- 1 tablespoon unsalted butter

Seasonings & Sauces:
- ½ teaspoon salt
- ¼ teaspoon black pepper
- ½ teaspoon garlic powder
- ½ teaspoon dried sage

Optional Additions:
- 1 teaspoon lemon zest for brightness
- ½ teaspoon Dijon mustard for depth

Nutritional Information
- **Calories:** 280 kcal
- **Carbs:** 1g
- **Fiber:** 0g
- **Protein:** 40g
- **Fats:** 12g
- **Sugar:** 0g

Instructions
1. **Preheat the Blackstone Griddle** to **medium heat** and lightly oil the surface.
2. Season turkey cutlets with salt, black pepper, garlic powder, and sage.
3. Cook for **3–4 minutes per side**, flipping once, until golden brown.
4. Add butter in the last minute and baste for extra flavor.

Chef's Tips: Pound turkey cutlets evenly for faster cooking.
Notes: Use fresh herbs for an aromatic touch.

Freedom Sizzling Lamb Chops

Prep Time: 10 minutes | **Cook Time:** 8 minutes | **Total Time:** 18 minutes

Ingredients
Main Ingredients:
- 4 small lamb chops (about 4 oz each)
- 1 tablespoon olive oil
- 1 tablespoon unsalted butter

Seasonings & Sauces:
- ½ teaspoon kosher salt
- ¼ teaspoon black pepper
- ½ teaspoon garlic powder
- ½ teaspoon dried rosemary
- ½ teaspoon lemon zest

Optional Additions:
- 1 teaspoon Dijon mustard for extra depth
- ½ teaspoon crushed red pepper for heat

Nutritional Information
- **Calories:** 380 kcal
- **Carbs:** 1g
- **Fiber:** 0g
- **Protein:** 40g
- **Fats:** 24g
- **Sugar:** 0g

Instructions
1. **Preheat the Blackstone Griddle** to **medium-high heat** and drizzle with olive oil.
2. Season lamb chops with salt, black pepper, garlic powder, rosemary, and lemon zest.
3. Sear for **3–4 minutes per side**, flipping once.
4. Add butter in the last minute and baste the chops.

Chef's Tips: Let lamb chops rest for 5 minutes before serving for best flavor.
Notes: Use fresh rosemary for an aromatic touch.

Founding Fathers' Bourbon-Glazed Chicken Breasts

Prep Time: 10 minutes | **Cook Time:** 12 minutes | **Total Time:** 22 minutes

Ingredients
Main Ingredients:
- 2 boneless, skinless chicken breasts
- 1 tablespoon olive oil
- 1 tablespoon unsalted butter

Seasonings & Sauces:
- ½ teaspoon salt
- ¼ teaspoon black pepper
- ½ teaspoon garlic powder
- ¼ cup bourbon
- 2 tablespoons brown sugar
- 1 teaspoon Dijon mustard

Optional Additions:
- ½ teaspoon smoked paprika
- ½ teaspoon Worcestershire sauce

Nutritional Information
- **Calories:** 420 kcal
- **Carbs:** 12g
- **Fiber:** 0g
- **Protein:** 40g
- **Fats:** 20g
- **Sugar:** 10g

Instructions
1. **Preheat the Blackstone Griddle** to **medium heat** and drizzle with olive oil.
2. Season chicken with salt, black pepper, and garlic powder.
3. Sear for **5–6 minutes per side**, flipping once.
4. In the last minute, brush with a glaze of bourbon, brown sugar, and mustard.

Chef's Tips: Cook bourbon glaze for 1 minute to reduce alcohol before brushing.
Notes: Omit bourbon for an alcohol-free version.

American Dream BBQ Pulled Pork Smash

Prep Time: 5 minutes | **Cook Time:** 10 minutes | **Total Time:** 15 minutes

Ingredients
Main Ingredients:
- ½ pound cooked pulled pork
- 2 brioche sandwich buns
- ¼ cup shredded cheddar cheese
- ¼ cup coleslaw

Seasonings & Sauces:
- ¼ cup BBQ sauce
- ½ teaspoon smoked paprika
- ¼ teaspoon black pepper
- 1 tablespoon apple cider vinegar

Optional Additions:
- 1 teaspoon hot sauce for extra heat
- ½ teaspoon honey for sweetness

Nutritional Information
- **Calories:** 550 kcal
- **Carbs:** 45g
- **Fiber:** 3g
- **Protein:** 35g
- **Fats:** 28g
- **Sugar:** 15g

Instructions
1. **Preheat the Blackstone Griddle** to **medium heat** and lightly oil the surface.
2. Toss pulled pork with BBQ sauce, smoked paprika, and black pepper.
3. Cook pork for **4–5 minutes**, stirring occasionally.
4. Toast buns on the griddle for **30 seconds**, then assemble with pork, cheese, and coleslaw.

Chef's Tips: Use leftover pulled pork for an easy meal.
Notes: Swap brioche for pretzel buns for a heartier option.

Patriot-Style Teriyaki Beef Tips

Prep Time: 10 minutes | **Cook Time:** 8 minutes | **Total Time:** 18 minutes

Ingredients
Main Ingredients:
- ½ pound sirloin steak, cut into bite-sized pieces
- 1 tablespoon olive oil
- 1 tablespoon unsalted butter

Seasonings & Sauces:
- ½ teaspoon salt
- ¼ teaspoon black pepper
- ½ teaspoon garlic powder
- ¼ cup teriyaki sauce
- 1 teaspoon sesame oil

Optional Additions:
- 1 teaspoon sesame seeds
- 1 tablespoon sliced green onions

Nutritional Information
- **Calories:** 390 kcal
- **Carbs:** 10g
- **Fiber:** 0g
- **Protein:** 40g
- **Fats:** 22g
- **Sugar:** 7g

Instructions
1. **Preheat the Blackstone Griddle** to **medium-high heat** and drizzle with oil.
2. Season beef tips with salt, black pepper, and garlic powder.
3. Cook for **3–4 minutes per side**, flipping once.
4. In the last minute, toss with teriyaki sauce and sesame oil.

Chef's Tips: Let beef rest for 5 minutes before serving for juicier meat.
Notes: Use tamari instead of teriyaki sauce for a gluten-free version.

Smoky Appalachian Griddle-Seared Ham Slices

Prep Time: 5 minutes | **Cook Time:** 6 minutes | **Total Time:** 11 minutes

Ingredients
Main Ingredients:
- 2 (4 oz) thick-cut ham slices
- 1 tablespoon unsalted butter
- 1 teaspoon olive oil

Seasonings & Sauces:
- ½ teaspoon brown sugar
- ½ teaspoon smoked paprika
- ¼ teaspoon black pepper
- ¼ teaspoon Dijon mustard

Optional Additions:
- 1 teaspoon apple cider vinegar
- 1 tablespoon chopped parsley

Nutritional Information
- **Calories:** 320 kcal
- **Carbs:** 5g
- **Fiber:** 0g
- **Protein:** 35g
- **Fats:** 16g
- **Sugar:** 3g

Instructions
1. **Preheat the Blackstone Griddle** to **medium heat** and add butter.
2. Season ham slices with brown sugar, smoked paprika, and black pepper.
3. Cook for **2–3 minutes per side**, flipping once.
4. In the last minute, brush with Dijon mustard and apple cider vinegar.

Chef's Tips: Use thick-cut ham for best texture and caramelization.
Notes: Swap butter for olive oil for a lighter version.

Crispy Liberty Fried Chicken Cutlets

Prep Time: 10 minutes | **Cook Time:** 12 minutes | **Total Time:** 22 minutes

Ingredients
Main Ingredients:
- 2 boneless, skinless chicken breasts, pounded thin
- ½ cup all-purpose flour
- ½ cup panko breadcrumbs
- 1 egg, beaten

Seasonings & Sauces:
- ½ teaspoon salt
- ½ teaspoon black pepper
- ½ teaspoon smoked paprika
- ½ teaspoon garlic powder
- ¼ teaspoon cayenne pepper

Optional Additions:
- 1 teaspoon Dijon mustard mixed into egg wash
- 1 tablespoon grated Parmesan for extra crisp

Nutritional Information
- **Calories:** 420 kcal
- **Carbs:** 35g
- **Fiber:** 2g
- **Protein:** 38g
- **Fats:** 14g
- **Sugar:** 1g

Instructions
1. **Preheat the Blackstone Griddle** to **medium heat** and drizzle with oil.
2. Dredge chicken in flour, dip in egg, then coat in panko mixed with seasonings.
3. Cook for **5–6 minutes per side**, flipping once, until crispy and golden brown.
4. Remove from heat and let rest for **2 minutes** before serving.

Chef's Tips: Press the breadcrumbs firmly for a crispier crust.
Notes: Use gluten-free flour and panko for a GF version.

Red, White & Blueberry-Glazed Pork Ribs

Prep Time: 10 minutes | **Cook Time:** 15 minutes | **Total Time:** 25 minutes

Ingredients
Main Ingredients:
- ½ rack baby back pork ribs, precooked and sliced
- 1 tablespoon olive oil
- ¼ cup blueberry preserves

Seasonings & Sauces:
- ½ teaspoon salt
- ½ teaspoon black pepper
- ½ teaspoon garlic powder
- ¼ teaspoon smoked paprika
- 1 teaspoon apple cider vinegar

Optional Additions:
- ½ teaspoon crushed red pepper for heat
- 1 teaspoon Dijon mustard for depth

Nutritional Information
- **Calories:** 480 kcal
- **Carbs:** 25g
- **Fiber:** 2g
- **Protein:** 40g
- **Fats:** 26g
- **Sugar:** 18g

Instructions
1. **Preheat the Blackstone Griddle** to **medium heat** and lightly oil the surface.
2. Season ribs with salt, black pepper, garlic powder, and smoked paprika.
3. Cook for **5 minutes per side**, brushing with blueberry glaze in the last 2 minutes.
4. Remove from heat and drizzle with apple cider vinegar before serving.

Chef's Tips: Use a melting dome to lock in moisture.
Notes: Swap blueberry preserves for cherry preserves for a different twist.

Firecracker Cajun-Spiced Chicken Wings

Prep Time: 10 minutes | **Cook Time:** 15 minutes | **Total Time:** 25 minutes

Ingredients
Main Ingredients:
- 8 chicken wings, split
- 1 tablespoon olive oil
- 1 tablespoon unsalted butter

Seasonings & Sauces:
- ½ teaspoon salt
- ½ teaspoon black pepper
- ½ teaspoon smoked paprika
- ½ teaspoon garlic powder
- ½ teaspoon Cajun seasoning

Optional Additions:
- 1 teaspoon hot sauce for extra spice
- ½ teaspoon honey for a sweet-heat balance

Nutritional Information
- **Calories:** 420 kcal
- **Carbs:** 3g
- **Fiber:** 1g
- **Protein:** 38g
- **Fats:** 28g
- **Sugar:** 2g

Instructions
1. **Preheat the Blackstone Griddle** to **medium-high heat** and lightly oil the surface.
2. Toss chicken wings with salt, black pepper, paprika, garlic powder, and Cajun seasoning.
3. Cook for **7–8 minutes per side**, flipping occasionally.
4. Toss in butter and hot sauce before serving.

Chef's Tips: Cover with a melting dome for even cooking.
Notes: Use smoked Cajun seasoning for a bolder taste.

Homestyle Blackstone Griddled Meatballs

Prep Time: 10 minutes | **Cook Time:** 10 minutes | **Total Time:** 20 minutes

Ingredients
Main Ingredients:
- ½ pound ground beef (80/20)
- ¼ cup breadcrumbs
- 1 egg, beaten
- 1 tablespoon grated Parmesan

Seasonings & Sauces:
- ½ teaspoon salt
- ¼ teaspoon black pepper
- ½ teaspoon garlic powder
- ½ teaspoon Italian seasoning

Optional Additions:
- 1 teaspoon Worcestershire sauce
- ¼ teaspoon crushed red pepper for spice

Nutritional Information
- **Calories:** 380 kcal
- **Carbs:** 12g
- **Fiber:** 1g
- **Protein:** 35g
- **Fats:** 22g
- **Sugar:** 2g

Instructions
1. **Preheat the Blackstone Griddle** to **medium heat** and lightly oil the surface.
2. Mix beef, breadcrumbs, egg, Parmesan, and seasonings, then shape into small meatballs.
3. Cook for **4–5 minutes per side**, turning occasionally for even browning.
4. Remove and let rest for **2 minutes** before serving.

Chef's Tips: Use an ice cream scoop for evenly sized meatballs.
Notes: Swap beef for turkey for a leaner version.

Texas Trail Smoked Brisket Slices

Prep Time: 5 minutes | **Cook Time:** 8 minutes | **Total Time:** 13 minutes

Ingredients
Main Ingredients:
- ½ pound cooked smoked brisket, sliced
- 1 tablespoon unsalted butter

Seasonings & Sauces:
- ½ teaspoon salt
- ¼ teaspoon black pepper
- ½ teaspoon smoked paprika
- ¼ teaspoon onion powder
- 2 tablespoons BBQ sauce

Optional Additions:
- 1 teaspoon apple cider vinegar for tang
- ½ teaspoon brown sugar for sweetness

Nutritional Information
- **Calories:** 480 kcal
- **Carbs:** 10g
- **Fiber:** 1g
- **Protein:** 45g
- **Fats:** 30g
- **Sugar:** 8g

Instructions
1. **Preheat the Blackstone Griddle** to **medium heat** and melt butter.
2. Season brisket slices with salt, black pepper, paprika, and onion powder.
3. Cook for **3–4 minutes per side**, flipping once.
4. Brush with BBQ sauce in the last minute and serve.

Chef's Tips: Use a griddle press for extra caramelization.
Notes: Serve with pickles and white bread for a Texas-style plate.

CHAPTER 6: GRILLED FISH & SEAFOOD

Liberty Bell Lemon Butter Salmon Fillets

Prep Time: 10 minutes | **Cook Time:** 8 minutes | **Total Time:** 18 minutes

Ingredients
Main Ingredients:
- 2 (6 oz) salmon fillets, skin-on
- 1 tablespoon olive oil
- 1 tablespoon unsalted butter

Seasonings & Sauces:
- ½ teaspoon kosher salt
- ¼ teaspoon black pepper
- ½ teaspoon garlic powder
- ½ teaspoon lemon zest
- 1 tablespoon fresh lemon juice

Optional Additions:
- 1 teaspoon chopped fresh parsley
- ½ teaspoon crushed red pepper for spice

Nutritional Information
- **Calories:** 420 kcal
- **Carbs:** 2g
- **Fiber:** 0g
- **Protein:** 45g
- **Fats:** 24g
- **Sugar:** 0g

Instructions
1. **Preheat the Blackstone Griddle** to **medium heat** and drizzle with olive oil.
2. Season salmon fillets with salt, black pepper, garlic powder, and lemon zest.
3. Place salmon skin-side down and cook for **4–5 minutes**, then flip and cook for **2–3 minutes** more.
4. In the last minute, add butter and lemon juice, basting the salmon.

Chef's Tips: Let the salmon cook undisturbed for crispier skin.
Notes: Use a spatula to carefully flip the fish to avoid breaking.

Stars & Stripes Cajun Shrimp Skewers

Prep Time: 10 minutes | **Cook Time:** 6 minutes | **Total Time:** 16 minutes

Ingredients
Main Ingredients:
- ½ pound large shrimp, peeled and deveined
- 2 wooden skewers, soaked in water
- 1 tablespoon olive oil

Seasonings & Sauces:
- ½ teaspoon Cajun seasoning
- ¼ teaspoon smoked paprika
- ¼ teaspoon black pepper
- ½ teaspoon garlic powder
- ½ teaspoon fresh lemon juice

Optional Additions:
- 1 teaspoon hot sauce for extra spice
- ½ teaspoon brown sugar for balance

Nutritional Information
- **Calories:** 220 kcal
- **Carbs:** 2g
- **Fiber:** 0g
- **Protein:** 30g
- **Fats:** 10g
- **Sugar:** 1g

Instructions
1. **Preheat the Blackstone Griddle** to **medium-high heat** and lightly oil the surface.
2. Toss shrimp with olive oil, Cajun seasoning, smoked paprika, and garlic powder.
3. Thread shrimp onto skewers and cook for **2–3 minutes per side**, flipping once.
4. In the last minute, drizzle with lemon juice and serve hot.

Chef's Tips: Use metal skewers for a reusable option.
Notes: Marinate shrimp for 10 minutes for deeper flavor.

1776 Garlic Butter Lobster Tails

Prep Time: 10 minutes | **Cook Time:** 8 minutes | **Total Time:** 18 minutes

Ingredients
Main Ingredients:
- 2 small lobster tails, split in half
- 1 tablespoon unsalted butter
- 1 teaspoon olive oil

Seasonings & Sauces:
- ½ teaspoon kosher salt
- ¼ teaspoon black pepper
- ½ teaspoon garlic powder
- ½ teaspoon lemon zest
- 1 teaspoon fresh lemon juice

Optional Additions:
- ½ teaspoon smoked paprika
- 1 teaspoon chopped fresh parsley

Nutritional Information
- **Calories:** 320 kcal
- **Carbs:** 1g
- **Fiber:** 0g
- **Protein:** 38g
- **Fats:** 18g
- **Sugar:** 0g

Instructions
1. **Preheat the Blackstone Griddle** to **medium heat** and lightly oil the surface.
2. Season lobster tails with salt, black pepper, garlic powder, and lemon zest.
3. Place lobster meat-side down and cook for **3–4 minutes**, then flip and cook another **3 minutes**.
4. In the last minute, baste with melted butter and lemon juice.

Chef's Tips: Use a sharp knife to split tails evenly for even cooking.
Notes: Serve with melted butter for dipping.

Frontier-Style Blackened Catfish

Prep Time: 10 minutes | **Cook Time:** 10 minutes | **Total Time:** 20 minutes

Ingredients
Main Ingredients:
- 2 (6 oz) catfish fillets
- 1 tablespoon olive oil
- 1 tablespoon unsalted butter

Seasonings & Sauces:
- ½ teaspoon salt
- ½ teaspoon black pepper
- ½ teaspoon smoked paprika
- ½ teaspoon garlic powder
- ¼ teaspoon cayenne pepper

Optional Additions:
- 1 teaspoon Worcestershire sauce
- ½ teaspoon lemon juice for tang

Nutritional Information
- **Calories:** 390 kcal
- **Carbs:** 3g
- **Fiber:** 1g
- **Protein:** 42g
- **Fats:** 22g
- **Sugar:** 1g

Instructions
1. **Preheat the Blackstone Griddle** to **medium-high heat** and drizzle with oil.
2. Coat catfish with salt, black pepper, paprika, garlic powder, and cayenne.
3. Cook for **4–5 minutes per side**, flipping once.
4. In the last minute, add butter and baste the fish.

Chef's Tips: Press fillets lightly to ensure even blackening.
Notes: Reduce cayenne if you prefer milder heat.

Smoky Appalachian Cedar-Plank Trout

Prep Time: 15 minutes | **Cook Time:** 12 minutes | **Total Time:** 27 minutes

Ingredients
Main Ingredients:
- 2 (6 oz) trout fillets
- 1 cedar plank, soaked in water for 1 hour
- 1 tablespoon olive oil

Seasonings & Sauces:
- ½ teaspoon salt
- ¼ teaspoon black pepper
- ½ teaspoon smoked paprika
- ½ teaspoon garlic powder
- 1 teaspoon fresh lemon juice

Optional Additions:
- 1 teaspoon Dijon mustard for tang
- ½ teaspoon chopped dill for freshness

Nutritional Information
- **Calories:** 350 kcal
- **Carbs:** 2g
- **Fiber:** 0g
- **Protein:** 40g
- **Fats:** 18g
- **Sugar:** 0g

Instructions
1. **Preheat the Blackstone Griddle** to **medium heat** and place the cedar plank on the surface.
2. Season trout with salt, black pepper, smoked paprika, and garlic powder.
3. Place trout skin-side down on the plank and cook for **10–12 minutes**.
4. Drizzle with lemon juice and remove from heat.

Chef's Tips: Soak cedar plank well to prevent burning.
Notes: Use a domed lid to trap heat for even cooking.

Uncle Sam's Classic Fish & Chips

Prep Time: 10 minutes | **Cook Time:** 15 minutes | **Total Time:** 25 minutes

Ingredients
Main Ingredients:
- 2 (6 oz) cod fillets
- 1 cup all-purpose flour
- ½ cup cornstarch
- ½ cup cold sparkling water
- 1 large russet potato, cut into fries

Seasonings & Sauces:
- ½ teaspoon salt
- ½ teaspoon black pepper
- ½ teaspoon smoked paprika
- ½ teaspoon garlic powder
- 1 tablespoon malt vinegar

Optional Additions:
- 1 teaspoon Old Bay seasoning for extra flavor
- ¼ cup tartar sauce for dipping

Nutritional Information
- **Calories:** 520 kcal
- **Carbs:** 68g
- **Fiber:** 5g
- **Protein:** 35g
- **Fats:** 14g
- **Sugar:** 2g

Instructions
1. **Preheat the Blackstone Griddle** to **medium heat** and lightly oil the surface.
2. Mix flour, cornstarch, smoked paprika, and sparkling water into a batter.
3. Coat fish in batter and cook for **4–5 minutes per side**, flipping once.
4. Cook fries separately for **8–10 minutes**, stirring occasionally.
5. Serve fish and chips with malt vinegar or tartar sauce.

Chef's Tips: Keep batter cold for the crispiest texture.
Notes: Swap cod for haddock for a different taste.

Great Plains Honey-Glazed Grilled Tilapia

Prep Time: 10 minutes | **Cook Time:** 8 minutes | **Total Time:** 18 minutes

Ingredients
Main Ingredients:
- 2 (6 oz) tilapia fillets
- 1 tablespoon olive oil
- 1 tablespoon honey

Seasonings & Sauces:
- ½ teaspoon salt
- ¼ teaspoon black pepper
- ½ teaspoon garlic powder
- ½ teaspoon smoked paprika
- 1 teaspoon fresh lemon juice

Optional Additions:
- ½ teaspoon Dijon mustard for balance
- 1 teaspoon fresh chopped cilantro

Nutritional Information
- **Calories:** 350 kcal
- **Carbs:** 12g
- **Fiber:** 0g
- **Protein:** 40g
- **Fats:** 15g
- **Sugar:** 9g

Instructions
1. **Preheat the Blackstone Griddle** to **medium-high heat** and lightly oil the surface.
2. Season tilapia with salt, black pepper, garlic powder, and smoked paprika.
3. Cook for **3–4 minutes per side**, flipping once.
4. In the last minute, brush with honey glaze and drizzle with lemon juice.

Chef's Tips: Use a thin spatula to prevent fillets from breaking.
Notes: Swap honey for maple syrup for a richer glaze.

American Dream Bourbon-Butter Scallops

Prep Time: 10 minutes | **Cook Time:** 6 minutes | **Total Time:** 16 minutes

Ingredients
Main Ingredients:
- 8 large sea scallops
- 1 tablespoon unsalted butter
- 1 teaspoon olive oil

Seasonings & Sauces:
- ½ teaspoon salt
- ¼ teaspoon black pepper
- ½ teaspoon garlic powder
- 2 tablespoons bourbon
- 1 teaspoon brown sugar

Optional Additions:
- ½ teaspoon crushed red pepper for heat
- 1 teaspoon fresh parsley for garnish

Nutritional Information
- **Calories:** 280 kcal
- **Carbs:** 5g
- **Fiber:** 0g
- **Protein:** 28g
- **Fats:** 12g
- **Sugar:** 4g

Instructions
1. **Preheat the Blackstone Griddle** to **medium-high heat** and drizzle with oil.
2. Season scallops with salt, black pepper, and garlic powder.
3. Sear for **2–3 minutes per side**, flipping once.
4. In the last minute, add butter, bourbon, and brown sugar, basting scallops.

Chef's Tips: Pat scallops dry for a better sear.
Notes: Use non-alcoholic vanilla extract instead of bourbon if preferred.

Buffalo Soldier Spicy Shrimp Tacos

Prep Time: 10 minutes | **Cook Time:** 8 minutes | **Total Time:** 18 minutes

Ingredients
Main Ingredients:
- ½ pound large shrimp, peeled and deveined
- 4 small corn tortillas
- 1 tablespoon olive oil
- ¼ cup shredded cabbage

Seasonings & Sauces:
- ½ teaspoon salt
- ¼ teaspoon black pepper
- ½ teaspoon smoked paprika
- ½ teaspoon garlic powder
- 2 tablespoons buffalo sauce

Optional Additions:
- 1 tablespoon crumbled queso fresco
- ½ teaspoon lime juice for zest

Nutritional Information
- **Calories:** 380 kcal
- **Carbs:** 38g
- **Fiber:** 5g
- **Protein:** 32g
- **Fats:** 12g
- **Sugar:** 3g

Instructions
1. **Preheat the Blackstone Griddle** to **medium heat** and lightly oil the surface.
2. Toss shrimp with salt, black pepper, smoked paprika, and garlic powder.
3. Cook for **2–3 minutes per side**, then toss in buffalo sauce.
4. Warm tortillas, assemble with shrimp, cabbage, and queso fresco.

Chef's Tips: Use charred tortillas for a smoky flavor.
Notes: Swap buffalo sauce for chipotle mayo for a milder heat.

Southern Glory Crispy Cornmeal Fried Fish

Prep Time: 10 minutes | **Cook Time:** 10 minutes | **Total Time:** 20 minutes

Ingredients
Main Ingredients:
- 2 (6 oz) white fish fillets (catfish or cod)
- ½ cup cornmeal
- ¼ cup all-purpose flour
- 1 egg, beaten

Seasonings & Sauces:
- ½ teaspoon salt
- ½ teaspoon black pepper
- ½ teaspoon smoked paprika
- ½ teaspoon garlic powder
- ½ teaspoon Cajun seasoning

Optional Additions:
- 1 teaspoon hot sauce for the egg wash
- 1 tablespoon tartar sauce for dipping

Nutritional Information
- **Calories:** 430 kcal
- **Carbs:** 38g
- **Fiber:** 4g
- **Protein:** 40g
- **Fats:** 14g
- **Sugar:** 2g

Instructions
1. **Preheat the Blackstone Griddle** to **medium heat** and lightly oil the surface.
2. Dredge fish in flour, dip in egg, then coat in cornmeal and seasoning mix.
3. Cook for **4–5 minutes per side**, flipping once.
4. Remove and serve with tartar sauce.

Chef's Tips: Let coated fish rest for 5 minutes before cooking for better adhesion.
Notes: Use gluten-free flour and cornmeal for a GF version.

Westward Ho' Griddled Garlic Butter Clams

Prep Time: 10 minutes | **Cook Time:** 8 minutes | **Total Time:** 18 minutes

Ingredients
Main Ingredients:
- 12 fresh littleneck clams, scrubbed
- 1 tablespoon unsalted butter
- 1 teaspoon olive oil

Seasonings & Sauces:
- ½ teaspoon salt
- ¼ teaspoon black pepper
- ½ teaspoon garlic powder
- ½ teaspoon red pepper flakes
- 1 tablespoon fresh lemon juice

Optional Additions:
- 1 teaspoon chopped parsley for garnish
- ½ teaspoon Worcestershire sauce for depth

Nutritional Information
- **Calories:** 180 kcal
- **Carbs:** 6g
- **Fiber:** 0g
- **Protein:** 22g
- **Fats:** 6g
- **Sugar:** 1g

Instructions
1. **Preheat the Blackstone Griddle** to **medium heat** and add olive oil.
2. Place clams directly on the griddle and cook for **6–8 minutes**, covered, until they open.
3. Melt butter on the griddle and mix with garlic powder, red pepper flakes, and lemon juice.
4. Drizzle over clams and serve hot.

Chef's Tips: Discard any clams that do not open.
Notes: Serve with crusty bread for soaking up the buttery sauce.

The Founding Fathers' Seafood Paella Skillet

Prep Time: 15 minutes | **Cook Time:** 20 minutes | **Total Time:** 35 minutes

Ingredients
Main Ingredients:
- ½ cup Arborio rice
- ½ pound mixed seafood (shrimp, mussels, clams)
- ½ cup chicken broth
- ¼ cup diced tomatoes
- ½ small onion, diced
- ½ small bell pepper, diced

Seasonings & Sauces:
- ½ teaspoon salt
- ¼ teaspoon black pepper
- ½ teaspoon smoked paprika
- ½ teaspoon saffron threads (optional)
- 1 teaspoon olive oil

Optional Additions:
- ½ teaspoon cayenne for heat
- 1 tablespoon chopped fresh parsley

Nutritional Information
- **Calories:** 420 kcal
- **Carbs:** 50g
- **Fiber:** 4g
- **Protein:** 32g
- **Fats:** 12g
- **Sugar:** 6g

Instructions
1. **Preheat the Blackstone Griddle** to **medium heat** and drizzle with olive oil.
2. Sauté onions and bell peppers for **2–3 minutes**, then add rice and cook for another **2 minutes**.
3. Pour in chicken broth, diced tomatoes, saffron, and seasonings, stirring occasionally.
4. Add seafood, cover, and cook for **6–8 minutes** until mussels and clams open.

Chef's Tips: Use pre-cooked rice for a quicker version.
Notes: Substitute saffron with turmeric for a budget-friendly option.

Freedom Firecracker Grilled Mahi-Mahi

Prep Time: 10 minutes | **Cook Time:** 8 minutes | **Total Time:** 18 minutes

Ingredients
Main Ingredients:
- 2 (6 oz) mahi-mahi fillets
- 1 tablespoon olive oil
- 1 tablespoon unsalted butter

Seasonings & Sauces:
- ½ teaspoon salt
- ¼ teaspoon black pepper
- ½ teaspoon smoked paprika
- ½ teaspoon garlic powder
- ½ teaspoon chili powder

Optional Additions:
- ½ teaspoon honey for balance
- 1 teaspoon fresh lime juice

Nutritional Information
- **Calories:** 350 kcal
- **Carbs:** 2g
- **Fiber:** 0g
- **Protein:** 42g
- **Fats:** 16g
- **Sugar:** 1g

Instructions
1. **Preheat the Blackstone Griddle** to **medium-high heat** and drizzle with oil.
2. Season mahi-mahi with salt, pepper, paprika, garlic powder, and chili powder.
3. Cook for **3–4 minutes per side**, flipping once.
4. In the last minute, add butter, honey, and lime juice, basting the fish.

Chef's Tips: Use a fish spatula for easy flipping.
Notes: Serve with grilled vegetables or mango salsa.

Patriot-Style Old Bay Crab Cakes

Prep Time: 15 minutes | **Cook Time:** 8 minutes | **Total Time:** 23 minutes

Ingredients

Main Ingredients:
- ½ pound lump crab meat
- ¼ cup breadcrumbs
- 1 egg, beaten
- 1 tablespoon mayonnaise

Seasonings & Sauces:
- ½ teaspoon Old Bay seasoning
- ¼ teaspoon salt
- ¼ teaspoon black pepper
- ½ teaspoon Dijon mustard
- ½ teaspoon Worcestershire sauce

Optional Additions:
- 1 teaspoon chopped fresh parsley
- ½ teaspoon hot sauce for spice

Nutritional Information
- **Calories:** 280 kcal
- **Carbs:** 14g
- **Fiber:** 1g
- **Protein:** 30g
- **Fats:** 12g
- **Sugar:** 1g

Instructions
1. **Preheat the Blackstone Griddle** to **medium heat** and lightly oil the surface.
2. Mix crab meat, breadcrumbs, egg, mayo, and seasonings in a bowl.
3. Form into two patties and place on the griddle.
4. Cook for **3–4 minutes per side**, flipping once.

Chef's Tips: Chill crab mixture for 10 minutes before cooking to hold shape.
Notes: Use gluten-free breadcrumbs for a GF version.

Red, White & Blueberry-Glazed Salmon Steaks

Prep Time: 10 minutes | **Cook Time:** 10 minutes | **Total Time:** 20 minutes

Ingredients
Main Ingredients:
- 2 (6 oz) salmon steaks
- 1 tablespoon olive oil
- 1 tablespoon unsalted butter

Seasonings & Sauces:
- ½ teaspoon salt
- ¼ teaspoon black pepper
- ½ teaspoon smoked paprika
- ¼ cup fresh blueberries
- 1 tablespoon balsamic vinegar

Optional Additions:
- ½ teaspoon honey for balance
- ½ teaspoon Dijon mustard for depth

Nutritional Information
- **Calories:** 420 kcal
- **Carbs:** 12g
- **Fiber:** 1g
- **Protein:** 45g
- **Fats:** 20g
- **Sugar:** 9g

Instructions
1. **Preheat the Blackstone Griddle** to **medium heat** and lightly oil the surface.
2. Season salmon steaks with salt, black pepper, and smoked paprika.
3. Cook for **4–5 minutes per side**, flipping once.
4. In the last minute, melt butter and add blueberries and balsamic vinegar, spooning over salmon.

Chef's Tips: Let salmon rest for 2 minutes before serving for best texture.
Notes: Swap blueberries for raspberries for a tangier glaze.

Texas Trail Chili-Lime Shrimp Fajitas

Prep Time: 10 minutes | **Cook Time:** 8 minutes | **Total Time:** 18 minutes

Ingredients
Main Ingredients:
- ½ pound large shrimp, peeled and deveined
- ½ small red bell pepper, sliced
- ½ small green bell pepper, sliced
- ½ small red onion, sliced
- 4 small flour tortillas

Seasonings & Sauces:
- ½ teaspoon salt
- ¼ teaspoon black pepper
- ½ teaspoon smoked paprika
- ½ teaspoon chili powder
- 1 teaspoon fresh lime juice

Optional Additions:
- 1 teaspoon chopped fresh cilantro
- ½ teaspoon crushed red pepper for spice

Nutritional Information
- **Calories:** 380 kcal
- **Carbs:** 42g
- **Fiber:** 5g
- **Protein:** 32g
- **Fats:** 10g
- **Sugar:** 6g

Instructions
1. **Preheat the Blackstone Griddle** to **medium-high heat** and drizzle with oil.
2. Toss shrimp with salt, black pepper, smoked paprika, chili powder, and lime juice.
3. Cook shrimp and vegetables for **3–4 minutes per side**, stirring occasionally.
4. Warm tortillas on the griddle, then assemble fajitas with shrimp and vegetables.

Chef's Tips: Serve with guacamole or salsa for added flavor.
Notes: Swap flour tortillas for corn tortillas for a GF option.

Homestyle Blackstone Griddled Swordfish Steaks

Prep Time: 10 minutes | **Cook Time:** 10 minutes | **Total Time:** 20 minutes

Ingredients
Main Ingredients:
- 2 (6 oz) swordfish steaks
- 1 tablespoon olive oil
- 1 tablespoon unsalted butter

Seasonings & Sauces:
- ½ teaspoon salt
- ¼ teaspoon black pepper
- ½ teaspoon garlic powder
- ½ teaspoon dried oregano
- 1 teaspoon lemon juice

Optional Additions:
- 1 teaspoon balsamic glaze for extra depth
- ½ teaspoon crushed red pepper for spice

Nutritional Information
- **Calories:** 420 kcal
- **Carbs:** 2g
- **Fiber:** 0g
- **Protein:** 45g
- **Fats:** 20g
- **Sugar:** 0g

Instructions
1. **Preheat the Blackstone Griddle** to **medium heat** and lightly oil the surface.
2. Season swordfish with salt, black pepper, garlic powder, and oregano.
3. Cook for **4–5 minutes per side**, flipping once.
4. In the last minute, add butter and lemon juice, basting the fish.

Chef's Tips: Use a fish spatula to prevent breaking.
Notes: Serve with grilled asparagus or a light salad.

Smoky BBQ Bacon-Wrapped Scallops

Prep Time: 10 minutes | **Cook Time:** 8 minutes | **Total Time:** 18 minutes

Ingredients
Main Ingredients:
- 6 large sea scallops
- 3 slices bacon, cut in half
- 1 tablespoon olive oil

Seasonings & Sauces:
- ½ teaspoon salt
- ¼ teaspoon black pepper
- ½ teaspoon smoked paprika
- 1 tablespoon BBQ sauce

Optional Additions:
- ½ teaspoon honey for caramelization
- 1 teaspoon fresh parsley for garnish

Nutritional Information
- **Calories:** 320 kcal
- **Carbs:** 4g
- **Fiber:** 0g
- **Protein:** 32g
- **Fats:** 18g
- **Sugar:** 3g

Instructions
1. **Preheat the Blackstone Griddle** to **medium heat** and lightly oil the surface.
2. Wrap each scallop with half a slice of bacon and secure with a toothpick.
3. Cook for **3–4 minutes per side**, flipping once.
4. In the last minute, brush with BBQ sauce and let caramelize.

Chef's Tips: Partially cook bacon before wrapping for crispier results.
Notes: Serve with a squeeze of lemon for balance.

Fire-Roasted Garlic Parmesan Oysters

Prep Time: 10 minutes | **Cook Time:** 10 minutes | **Total Time:** 20 minutes

Ingredients
Main Ingredients:
- 6 fresh oysters, shucked
- 1 tablespoon unsalted butter
- 1 tablespoon grated Parmesan cheese

Seasonings & Sauces:
- ½ teaspoon salt
- ¼ teaspoon black pepper
- ½ teaspoon garlic powder
- ½ teaspoon smoked paprika
- 1 teaspoon fresh lemon juice

Optional Additions:
- ½ teaspoon red pepper flakes for heat
- 1 teaspoon chopped fresh parsley

Nutritional Information
- **Calories:** 220 kcal
- **Carbs:** 4g
- **Fiber:** 0g
- **Protein:** 20g
- **Fats:** 12g
- **Sugar:** 0g

Instructions
1. **Preheat the Blackstone Griddle** to **medium heat** and lightly oil the surface.
2. Place oysters directly on the griddle and cook for **5–6 minutes**, until juices start to bubble.
3. Add butter, garlic powder, smoked paprika, and Parmesan.
4. Cook for another **2 minutes**, then drizzle with lemon juice before serving.

Chef's Tips: Use a melting dome for even cooking.
Notes: Serve with toasted bread for dipping.

New England-Style Lobster Roll Sliders

Prep Time: 15 minutes | **Cook Time:** 5 minutes | **Total Time:** 20 minutes

Ingredients
Main Ingredients:
- ½ pound cooked lobster meat, chopped
- 2 small brioche slider buns
- 1 tablespoon unsalted butter

Seasonings & Sauces:
- 1 tablespoon mayonnaise
- ½ teaspoon Dijon mustard
- ½ teaspoon fresh lemon juice
- ¼ teaspoon salt
- ¼ teaspoon black pepper

Optional Additions:
- 1 teaspoon chopped fresh chives
- ½ teaspoon Old Bay seasoning for extra flavor

Nutritional Information
- **Calories:** 420 kcal
- **Carbs:** 32g
- **Fiber:** 2g
- **Protein:** 35g
- **Fats:** 18g
- **Sugar:** 4g

Instructions
1. **Preheat the Blackstone Griddle** to **medium heat** and toast brioche buns with butter.
2. In a bowl, mix lobster meat with mayo, mustard, lemon juice, salt, and pepper.
3. Assemble sliders with the lobster mixture and serve warm.

Chef's Tips: Chill lobster salad before serving for better flavor.
Notes: Swap brioche buns for lettuce wraps for a low-carb version.

CHAPTER 7: BURGERS & GOURMET SANDWICHES

Liberty Bell Classic Smash Burger

Prep Time: 10 minutes | **Cook Time:** 6 minutes | **Total Time:** 16 minutes

Ingredients
Main Ingredients:
- ½ pound ground beef (80/20)
- 2 brioche buns
- 2 slices American cheese
- 1 tablespoon unsalted butter

Seasonings & Sauces:
- ½ teaspoon kosher salt
- ¼ teaspoon black pepper
- ½ teaspoon garlic powder
- 1 tablespoon burger sauce (mayo, ketchup, mustard blend)

Optional Additions:
- ¼ cup shredded lettuce
- 2 pickle slices

Nutritional Information
- **Calories:** 620 kcal
- **Carbs:** 38g
- **Fiber:** 2g
- **Protein:** 42g
- **Fats:** 35g
- **Sugar:** 6g

Instructions
1. **Preheat the Blackstone Griddle** to **medium-high heat** and butter the buns, toasting them for **1 minute**.
2. Divide beef into two balls and smash onto the hot griddle, pressing firmly for crisp edges.
3. Season patties and cook for **2–3 minutes per side**, flipping once.
4. Place cheese on patties, let melt, and assemble burgers with toppings and sauce.

Chef's Tips: Smash burgers cook best on a very hot griddle—don't press after flipping.
Notes: Swap brioche buns for potato rolls for a softer bite.

Stars & Stripes Bacon Cheddar BBQ Burger

Prep Time: 10 minutes | **Cook Time:** 8 minutes | **Total Time:** 18 minutes

Ingredients
Main Ingredients:
- ½ pound ground beef (80/20)
- 2 sesame seed buns
- 2 slices sharp cheddar cheese
- 2 strips crispy bacon

Seasonings & Sauces:
- ½ teaspoon salt
- ¼ teaspoon black pepper
- ½ teaspoon smoked paprika
- 2 tablespoons BBQ sauce

Optional Additions:
- 1 crispy onion ring
- 1 teaspoon chopped jalapeños

Nutritional Information
- **Calories:** 710 kcal
- **Carbs:** 40g
- **Fiber:** 2g
- **Protein:** 45g
- **Fats:** 42g
- **Sugar:** 8g

Instructions
1. **Preheat the Blackstone Griddle** to **medium heat** and toast buns with butter.
2. Form beef into two patties, season, and cook for **3–4 minutes per side**.
3. Add cheese, let melt, then stack with bacon, BBQ sauce, and optional toppings.

Chef's Tips: Use thick-cut bacon for extra crunch.
Notes: Swap cheddar for smoked gouda for deeper flavor.

1776 All-American Patty Melt

Prep Time: 10 minutes | **Cook Time:** 10 minutes | **Total Time:** 20 minutes

Ingredients
Main Ingredients:
- ½ pound ground beef
- 4 slices rye bread
- 4 slices Swiss cheese
- ½ small onion, caramelized

Seasonings & Sauces:
- ½ teaspoon salt
- ¼ teaspoon black pepper
- ½ teaspoon Worcestershire sauce
- 1 tablespoon unsalted butter

Optional Additions:
- 1 teaspoon Dijon mustard
- 1 teaspoon mayo

Nutritional Information
- **Calories:** 680 kcal
- **Carbs:** 48g
- **Fiber:** 4g
- **Protein:** 46g
- **Fats:** 32g
- **Sugar:** 6g

Instructions
1. **Preheat the Blackstone Griddle** to **medium heat** and butter the bread slices.
2. Form beef into two thin patties, season, and cook for **3 minutes per side**.
3. Layer Swiss cheese, caramelized onions, and patties between toasted bread, pressing down lightly.

Chef's Tips: Cook onions on low heat for 10 minutes for better caramelization.
Notes: Swap rye bread for Texas toast for a thicker bite.

Frontier-Style Bison Burger with Caramelized Onions

Prep Time: 10 minutes | **Cook Time:** 8 minutes | **Total Time:** 18 minutes

Ingredients
Main Ingredients:
- ½ pound ground bison
- 2 whole wheat buns
- 2 slices pepper jack cheese
- ½ small onion, caramelized

Seasonings & Sauces:
- ½ teaspoon salt
- ¼ teaspoon black pepper
- ½ teaspoon garlic powder
- 1 teaspoon Dijon mustard

Optional Additions:
- 1 teaspoon balsamic glaze
- ½ teaspoon hot sauce

Nutritional Information
- **Calories:** 610 kcal
- **Carbs:** 42g
- **Fiber:** 3g
- **Protein:** 48g
- **Fats:** 24g
- **Sugar:** 5g

Instructions
1. **Preheat the Blackstone Griddle** to **medium heat** and toast buns with butter.
2. Form bison into two patties, season, and cook for **4 minutes per side**.
3. Add cheese, let melt, then top with caramelized onions and balsamic glaze.

Chef's Tips: Don't overcook bison—it's leaner than beef and cooks quickly.
Notes: Swap whole wheat buns for brioche for a richer taste.

Smoky Appalachian Pulled Pork Sandwich

Prep Time: 10 minutes | **Cook Time:** 12 minutes | **Total Time:** 22 minutes

Ingredients
Main Ingredients:
- ½ pound cooked pulled pork
- 2 soft sandwich buns
- ¼ cup coleslaw

Seasonings & Sauces:
- ½ teaspoon smoked paprika
- ¼ teaspoon black pepper
- ½ teaspoon garlic powder
- 2 tablespoons BBQ sauce

Optional Additions:
- 1 teaspoon apple cider vinegar
- 1 teaspoon honey for sweetness

Nutritional Information
- **Calories:** 640 kcal
- **Carbs:** 45g
- **Fiber:** 3g
- **Protein:** 42g
- **Fats:** 28g
- **Sugar:** 14g

Instructions
1. **Preheat the Blackstone Griddle** to **medium heat** and warm the pulled pork for **5–6 minutes**, stirring occasionally.
2. Toast sandwich buns with butter, then stack with pork, BBQ sauce, and coleslaw.

Chef's Tips: Use a melting dome to keep pulled pork warm and moist.
Notes: Swap BBQ sauce for Carolina mustard sauce for a tangy twist.

Uncle Sam's Philly Cheesesteak Hoagie

Prep Time: 10 minutes | **Cook Time:** 8 minutes | **Total Time:** 18 minutes

Ingredients
Main Ingredients:
- ½ pound thinly sliced ribeye steak
- 1 small hoagie roll
- ½ small onion, sliced
- ½ small green bell pepper, sliced
- 2 slices provolone cheese

Seasonings & Sauces:
- ½ teaspoon salt
- ¼ teaspoon black pepper
- ½ teaspoon garlic powder
- 1 tablespoon Worcestershire sauce

Optional Additions:
- 1 teaspoon mayo
- ½ teaspoon crushed red pepper for heat

Nutritional Information
- **Calories:** 630 kcal
- **Carbs:** 44g
- **Fiber:** 3g
- **Protein:** 45g
- **Fats:** 28g
- **Sugar:** 5g

Instructions
1. **Preheat the Blackstone Griddle** to **medium heat** and lightly oil the surface.
2. Sauté onions and peppers for **3–4 minutes**, then move to the side.
3. Cook steak for **3–4 minutes**, seasoning with salt, pepper, and Worcestershire sauce.
4. Layer cheese over steak, let melt, then load into a toasted hoagie roll.

Chef's Tips: Use ribeye for the juiciest, most flavorful cheesesteak.
Notes: Swap provolone for Cheez Whiz for a classic Philly twist.

Great Plains Juicy Lucy Stuffed Burger

P rep Time: 10 minutes | **Cook Time:** 8 minutes | **Total Time:** 18 minutes

Ingredients
Main Ingredients:
- ½ pound ground beef (80/20)
- 2 sesame seed buns
- 2 ounces cheddar cheese, cubed

Seasonings & Sauces:
- ½ teaspoon salt
- ¼ teaspoon black pepper
- ½ teaspoon garlic powder
- ½ teaspoon onion powder

Optional Additions:
- 1 teaspoon burger sauce
- 1 teaspoon diced jalapeños for spice

Nutritional Information
- **Calories:** 690 kcal
- **Carbs:** 40g
- **Fiber:** 2g
- **Protein:** 48g
- **Fats:** 38g
- **Sugar:** 5g

Instructions
1. **Preheat the Blackstone Griddle** to **medium-high heat** and toast the buns.
2. Form two beef patties and press a cheese cube into the center of one, sealing with the other.
3. Cook for **4 minutes per side**, flipping once, until cheese is melted inside.
4. Assemble burger with toppings and sauce.

Chef's Tips: Let the burger rest for a minute to avoid cheese spilling out.
Notes: Swap cheddar for pepper jack for extra spice.

American Dream Fried Chicken Sandwich

Prep Time: 15 minutes | **Cook Time:** 10 minutes | **Total Time:** 25 minutes

Ingredients
Main Ingredients:
- 2 boneless, skinless chicken thighs
- ½ cup buttermilk
- ½ cup all-purpose flour
- 2 brioche buns

Seasonings & Sauces:
- ½ teaspoon salt
- ½ teaspoon black pepper
- ½ teaspoon garlic powder
- ½ teaspoon smoked paprika
- 1 tablespoon mayo

Optional Additions:
- 1 teaspoon hot sauce
- 2 pickle slices

Nutritional Information
- **Calories:** 750 kcal
- **Carbs:** 55g
- **Fiber:** 3g
- **Protein:** 52g
- **Fats:** 35g
- **Sugar:** 6g

Instructions
1. **Preheat the Blackstone Griddle** to **medium heat** and lightly oil the surface.
2. Dredge chicken in buttermilk, then coat in seasoned flour.
3. Fry for **5–6 minutes per side**, flipping once, until golden and crispy.
4. Assemble sandwich with mayo and pickles.

Chef's Tips: Use cornstarch in the flour mix for extra crunch.
Notes: Swap brioche buns for potato buns for a softer bite.

Buffalo Soldier Spicy Chicken Ranch Burger

Prep Time: 10 minutes | **Cook Time:** 10 minutes | **Total Time:** 20 minutes

Ingredients
Main Ingredients:
- ½ pound ground chicken
- 2 brioche buns
- 2 slices pepper jack cheese

Seasonings & Sauces:
- ½ teaspoon salt
- ¼ teaspoon black pepper
- ½ teaspoon garlic powder
- ½ teaspoon smoked paprika
- 2 tablespoons buffalo sauce

Optional Additions:
- 1 tablespoon ranch dressing
- ¼ cup shredded lettuce

Nutritional Information
- **Calories:** 640 kcal
- **Carbs:** 40g
- **Fiber:** 2g
- **Protein:** 50g
- **Fats:** 28g
- **Sugar:** 4g

Instructions
1. **Preheat the Blackstone Griddle** to **medium-high heat** and toast the buns.
2. Form ground chicken into two patties, season, and cook for **4–5 minutes per side**.
3. Add cheese and let melt, then brush patties with buffalo sauce.
4. Assemble burger with ranch dressing and lettuce.

Chef's Tips: Mix a little ranch into the buffalo sauce for balance.
Notes: Use blue cheese crumbles instead of ranch for a bold twist.

Southern Glory Buttermilk Biscuit Sausage Sandwich

Prep Time: 15 minutes | **Cook Time:** 10 minutes | **Total Time:** 25 minutes

Ingredients
Main Ingredients:
- 2 large buttermilk biscuits
- 2 sausage patties
- 1 slice cheddar cheese

Seasonings & Sauces:
- ½ teaspoon salt
- ¼ teaspoon black pepper
- ½ teaspoon garlic powder
- ½ teaspoon maple syrup

Optional Additions:
- 1 fried egg
- 1 teaspoon hot honey

Nutritional Information
- **Calories:** 580 kcal
- **Carbs:** 45g
- **Fiber:** 3g
- **Protein:** 38g
- **Fats:** 28g
- **Sugar:** 7g

Instructions
1. **Preheat the Blackstone Griddle** to **medium heat** and lightly oil the surface.
2. Cook sausage patties for **4 minutes per side**, flipping once.
3. Toast biscuits on the griddle, then assemble with sausage, cheese, and optional toppings.

Chef's Tips: Use freshly baked biscuits for best texture.
Notes: Swap cheddar for pimento cheese for a Southern twist.

Westward Ho' BBQ Brisket Sliders

Prep Time: 10 minutes | **Cook Time:** 8 minutes | **Total Time:** 18 minutes

Ingredients
Main Ingredients:
- ½ pound cooked smoked brisket, sliced thin
- 4 small slider buns
- ¼ cup coleslaw

Seasonings & Sauces:
- ½ teaspoon salt
- ¼ teaspoon black pepper
- ½ teaspoon smoked paprika
- 2 tablespoons BBQ sauce

Optional Additions:
- ½ teaspoon hot sauce for spice
- 1 teaspoon honey for sweetness

Nutritional Information
- **Calories:** 520 kcal
- **Carbs:** 45g
- **Fiber:** 3g
- **Protein:** 42g
- **Fats:** 24g
- **Sugar:** 10g

Instructions
1. **Preheat the Blackstone Griddle** to **medium heat** and lightly oil the surface.
2. Warm sliced brisket for **3–4 minutes**, flipping occasionally.
3. Toast slider buns for **1 minute**, then layer with brisket, BBQ sauce, and coleslaw.

Chef's Tips: Use a melting dome to keep brisket warm and juicy.
Notes: Swap BBQ sauce for Carolina mustard sauce for a tangy twist.

The Founding Fathers' Classic Reuben

Prep Time: 10 minutes | **Cook Time:** 8 minutes | **Total Time:** 18 minutes

Ingredients
Main Ingredients:
- 4 slices rye bread
- ½ pound sliced corned beef
- 4 slices Swiss cheese
- ¼ cup sauerkraut

Seasonings & Sauces:
- ½ teaspoon salt
- ¼ teaspoon black pepper
- 1 tablespoon Russian dressing

Optional Additions:
- 1 teaspoon horseradish for extra kick
- 1 tablespoon butter for toasting

Nutritional Information
- **Calories:** 650 kcal
- **Carbs:** 48g
- **Fiber:** 4g
- **Protein:** 42g
- **Fats:** 28g
- **Sugar:** 4g

Instructions
1. **Preheat the Blackstone Griddle** to **medium heat** and butter the bread slices.
2. Stack corned beef, Swiss cheese, and sauerkraut between the bread, spreading Russian dressing on one side.
3. Grill sandwich for **3–4 minutes per side**, pressing down lightly for crispiness.

Chef's Tips: Press with a spatula for a crispier crust.
Notes: Swap Russian dressing for Thousand Island for a milder flavor.

Freedom Fire-Grilled Turkey Club

P rep Time: 10 minutes | **Cook Time:** 8 minutes | **Total Time:** 18 minutes

Ingredients
Main Ingredients:
- 6 slices turkey breast
- 3 slices sourdough bread
- 2 slices crispy bacon
- 2 slices cheddar cheese
- 2 slices tomato
- ¼ cup shredded lettuce

Seasonings & Sauces:
- ½ teaspoon salt
- ¼ teaspoon black pepper
- 1 tablespoon mayo

Optional Additions:
- ½ teaspoon Dijon mustard for extra tang
- 1 teaspoon honey for sweetness

Nutritional Information
- **Calories:** 680 kcal
- **Carbs:** 50g
- **Fiber:** 5g
- **Protein:** 46g
- **Fats:** 28g
- **Sugar:** 6g

Instructions
1. **Preheat the Blackstone Griddle** to **medium heat** and toast the sourdough slices with butter.
2. Stack turkey, cheese, bacon, tomato, and lettuce between the toasted bread, spreading mayo on each slice.
3. Grill sandwich for **2 minutes per side**, pressing gently.

Chef's Tips: Use a serrated knife to slice cleanly.
Notes: Swap cheddar for Swiss for a milder taste.

Patriot-Style Triple-Decker Grilled Cheese

Prep Time: 10 minutes | **Cook Time:** 6 minutes | **Total Time:** 16 minutes

Ingredients
Main Ingredients:
- 6 slices thick-cut white bread
- 2 slices cheddar cheese
- 2 slices Swiss cheese
- 2 slices pepper jack cheese

Seasonings & Sauces:
- 1 teaspoon unsalted butter
- ½ teaspoon garlic powder

Optional Additions:
- ½ teaspoon red pepper flakes for heat
- 1 teaspoon Dijon mustard for extra tang

Nutritional Information
- **Calories:** 740 kcal
- **Carbs:** 48g
- **Fiber:** 4g
- **Protein:** 40g
- **Fats:** 38g
- **Sugar:** 4g

Instructions
1. **Preheat the Blackstone Griddle** to **medium-low heat** and butter the bread slices.
2. Layer cheeses between bread, stacking three slices for a tall sandwich.
3. Grill for **3 minutes per side**, flipping once, until cheese melts.

Chef's Tips: Cover with a melting dome for even cheese melting.
Notes: Swap pepper jack for mozzarella for a milder bite.

Red, White & Blueberry BBQ Pulled Chicken Sandwich

Prep Time: 10 minutes | **Cook Time:** 10 minutes | **Total Time:** 20 minutes

Ingredients
Main Ingredients:
- ½ pound cooked pulled chicken
- 2 sandwich buns
- ¼ cup shredded coleslaw

Seasonings & Sauces:
- ½ teaspoon salt
- ¼ teaspoon black pepper
- ½ teaspoon smoked paprika
- 2 tablespoons blueberry BBQ sauce

Optional Additions:
- 1 teaspoon balsamic vinegar for extra tang
- 1 teaspoon honey for sweetness

Nutritional Information
- **Calories:** 580 kcal
- **Carbs:** 48g
- **Fiber:** 3g
- **Protein:** 44g
- **Fats:** 20g
- **Sugar:** 12g

Instructions
1. **Preheat the Blackstone Griddle** to **medium heat** and warm pulled chicken for **5 minutes**, stirring occasionally.
2. Toast sandwich buns, then assemble with pulled chicken, blueberry BBQ sauce, and coleslaw.

Chef's Tips: Use homemade blueberry BBQ sauce for a richer flavor.
Notes: Swap buns for Texas toast for a crunchier sandwich.

CHAPTER 8: RECIPES FOR SPECIAL OCCASIONS

Liberty Bell New Year's Eve Surf & Turf Platter

Prep Time: 15 minutes | **Cook Time:** 12 minutes | **Total Time:** 27 minutes

Ingredients
Main Ingredients:
- 1 (8 oz) filet mignon
- 6 large shrimp, peeled and deveined
- 1 tablespoon unsalted butter
- 1 teaspoon olive oil

Seasonings & Sauces:
- ½ teaspoon salt
- ¼ teaspoon black pepper
- ½ teaspoon garlic powder
- ½ teaspoon smoked paprika
- 1 teaspoon fresh lemon juice

Optional Additions:
- 1 teaspoon Worcestershire sauce for depth
- ½ teaspoon fresh chopped parsley for garnish

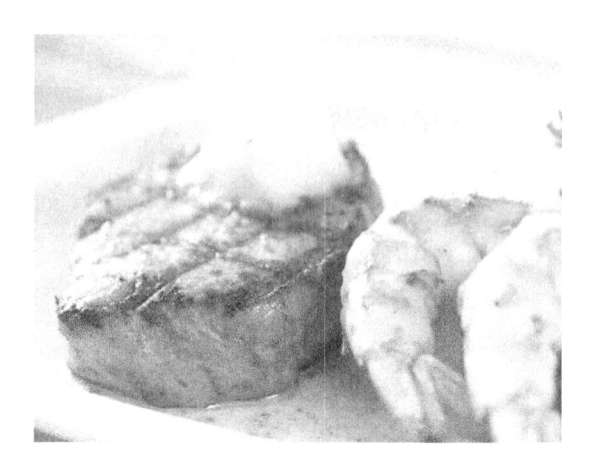

Nutritional Information
- **Calories:** 620 kcal
- **Carbs:** 4g
- **Fiber:** 0g
- **Protein:** 56g
- **Fats:** 38g
- **Sugar:** 1g

Instructions
1. **Preheat the Blackstone Griddle** to **medium-high heat** and lightly oil the surface.
2. Season the filet mignon and shrimp with salt, black pepper, smoked paprika, and garlic powder.
3. Sear steak for **4–5 minutes per side**, flipping once. Add shrimp to the griddle, cooking for **2–3 minutes per side**.
4. In the last minute, melt butter, mix with lemon juice, and baste both steak and shrimp.

Chef's Tips: Let steak rest for 5 minutes before slicing for better texture.
Notes: Swap filet mignon for ribeye for a juicier cut.

Stars & Stripes Fourth of July BBQ Ribs

Prep Time: 10 minutes | **Cook Time:** 15 minutes | **Total Time:** 25 minutes

Ingredients
Main Ingredients:
- ½ rack baby back ribs, precooked and sliced
- 1 tablespoon unsalted butter
- ¼ cup BBQ sauce

Seasonings & Sauces:
- ½ teaspoon salt
- ½ teaspoon black pepper
- ½ teaspoon smoked paprika
- ¼ teaspoon cayenne pepper

Optional Additions:
- 1 teaspoon apple cider vinegar for tang
- ½ teaspoon brown sugar for caramelization

Nutritional Information
- **Calories:** 540 kcal
- **Carbs:** 20g
- **Fiber:** 1g
- **Protein:** 48g
- **Fats:** 32g
- **Sugar:** 12g

Instructions
1. **Preheat the Blackstone Griddle** to **medium heat** and melt butter.
2. Season ribs with salt, black pepper, smoked paprika, and cayenne.
3. Cook for **5 minutes per side**, flipping once, brushing with BBQ sauce in the last 2 minutes.

Chef's Tips: Cover ribs with foil while cooking to keep them moist.
Notes: Use a basting brush to evenly coat ribs with sauce.

1776 Thanksgiving Griddled Turkey & Cranberry Sliders

Prep Time: 10 minutes | **Cook Time:** 10 minutes | **Total Time:** 20 minutes

Ingredients
Main Ingredients:
- ½ pound cooked turkey breast, sliced
- 4 small slider buns
- ¼ cup cranberry sauce

Seasonings & Sauces:
- ½ teaspoon salt
- ¼ teaspoon black pepper
- ½ teaspoon garlic powder
- 1 tablespoon mayonnaise

Optional Additions:
- 1 teaspoon Dijon mustard for extra tang
- ½ teaspoon fresh thyme for garnish

Nutritional Information
- **Calories:** 460 kcal
- **Carbs:** 42g
- **Fiber:** 3g
- **Protein:** 44g
- **Fats:** 14g
- **Sugar:** 8g

Instructions
1. **Preheat the Blackstone Griddle** to **medium heat** and lightly oil the surface.
2. Toast slider buns for **1 minute**, then layer turkey, cranberry sauce, and mayonnaise.
3. Grill sliders for **2 minutes per side**, pressing gently for crispiness.

Chef's Tips: Mix cranberry sauce with Dijon mustard for a bolder flavor.
Notes: Swap turkey for roasted chicken for a different variation.

Frontier-Style Cowboy Christmas Prime Rib

Prep Time: 15 minutes | **Cook Time:** 12 minutes | **Total Time:** 27 minutes

Ingredients
Main Ingredients:
- 1 (12 oz) prime rib steak
- 1 tablespoon unsalted butter
- 1 teaspoon olive oil

Seasonings & Sauces:
- ½ teaspoon salt
- ¼ teaspoon black pepper
- ½ teaspoon garlic powder
- ½ teaspoon dried rosemary

Optional Additions:
- 1 teaspoon Worcestershire sauce
- ½ teaspoon horseradish for serving

Nutritional Information
- **Calories:** 720 kcal
- **Carbs:** 3g
- **Fiber:** 0g
- **Protein:** 58g
- **Fats:** 48g
- **Sugar:** 1g

Instructions
1. **Preheat the Blackstone Griddle** to **medium-high heat** and drizzle with olive oil.
2. Season prime rib with salt, black pepper, garlic powder, and rosemary.
3. Sear for **5–6 minutes per side**, flipping once.
4. In the last minute, add butter and baste the steak for extra richness.

Chef's Tips: Let prime rib rest for 5–7 minutes before slicing.
Notes: Serve with horseradish sauce for a traditional pairing.

Smoky Appalachian Easter Honey-Glazed Ham

Prep Time: 10 minutes | **Cook Time:** 10 minutes | **Total Time:** 20 minutes

Ingredients
Main Ingredients:
- ½ pound thick-cut ham slices
- 1 tablespoon unsalted butter
- 1 teaspoon honey

Seasonings & Sauces:
- ½ teaspoon salt
- ¼ teaspoon black pepper
- ½ teaspoon smoked paprika
- ½ teaspoon Dijon mustard

Optional Additions:
- 1 teaspoon apple cider vinegar for extra depth
- ½ teaspoon brown sugar for sweetness

Nutritional Information
- **Calories:** 420 kcal
- **Carbs:** 12g
- **Fiber:** 0g
- **Protein:** 42g
- **Fats:** 20g
- **Sugar:** 10g

Instructions
1. **Preheat the Blackstone Griddle** to **medium heat** and melt butter.
2. Season ham slices with salt, black pepper, smoked paprika, and Dijon mustard.
3. Cook for **3–4 minutes per side**, flipping once.
4. In the last minute, drizzle with honey and apple cider vinegar.

Chef's Tips: Let honey glaze caramelize slightly for better flavor.
Notes: Serve with mashed sweet potatoes for a complete meal.

Uncle Sam's Memorial Day All-American Hot Dogs

Prep Time: 5 minutes | **Cook Time:** 8 minutes | **Total Time:** 13 minutes

Ingredients
Main Ingredients:
- 2 all-beef hot dogs
- 2 hot dog buns
- ¼ cup diced onions

Seasonings & Sauces:
- ½ teaspoon yellow mustard
- 1 tablespoon ketchup
- ½ teaspoon salt

Optional Additions:
- ¼ cup shredded cheddar cheese
- 1 teaspoon sweet relish

Nutritional Information
- **Calories:** 460 kcal
- **Carbs:** 38g
- **Fiber:** 3g
- **Protein:** 22g
- **Fats:** 26g
- **Sugar:** 8g

Instructions
1. **Preheat the Blackstone Griddle** to **medium heat** and lightly oil the surface.
2. Grill hot dogs for **3–4 minutes per side**, turning occasionally for even cooking.
3. Toast buns for **30 seconds**, then assemble with toppings and condiments.

Chef's Tips: Score hot dogs lightly before grilling for better texture.
Notes: Swap cheddar for pepper jack for a spicy kick.

Great Plains Father's Day Bourbon-Glazed Steak

Prep Time: 10 minutes | **Cook Time:** 10 minutes | **Total Time:** 20 minutes

Ingredients
Main Ingredients:
- 1 (10 oz) ribeye steak
- 1 tablespoon unsalted butter
- 1 teaspoon olive oil

Seasonings & Sauces:
- ½ teaspoon salt
- ¼ teaspoon black pepper
- ½ teaspoon garlic powder
- 2 tablespoons bourbon
- 1 teaspoon brown sugar

Optional Additions:
- 1 teaspoon Worcestershire sauce
- ½ teaspoon Dijon mustard for depth

Nutritional Information
- **Calories:** 720 kcal
- **Carbs:** 4g
- **Fiber:** 0g
- **Protein:** 54g
- **Fats:** 50g
- **Sugar:** 3g

Instructions
1. **Preheat the Blackstone Griddle** to **medium-high heat** and drizzle with olive oil.
2. Season steak with salt, black pepper, and garlic powder.
3. Sear for **5 minutes per side**, flipping once.
4. In the last minute, baste with melted butter, bourbon, and brown sugar.

Chef's Tips: Let steak rest for 5 minutes before slicing for maximum juiciness.
Notes: Use non-alcoholic vanilla extract instead of bourbon if preferred.

American Dream Mother's Day Strawberry Shortcake Pancakes

Prep Time: 10 minutes | **Cook Time:** 8 minutes | **Total Time:** 18 minutes

Ingredients
Main Ingredients:
- 1 cup pancake batter
- ½ cup sliced strawberries
- ¼ cup whipped cream

Seasonings & Sauces:
- ½ teaspoon vanilla extract
- 1 tablespoon maple syrup
- 1 teaspoon powdered sugar

Optional Additions:
- ½ teaspoon cinnamon for warmth
- 1 tablespoon crushed pecans for crunch

Nutritional Information
- **Calories:** 420 kcal
- **Carbs:** 60g
- **Fiber:** 4g
- **Protein:** 10g
- **Fats:** 12g
- **Sugar:** 18g

Instructions
1. **Preheat the Blackstone Griddle** to **medium heat** and lightly butter the surface.
2. Pour pancake batter onto the griddle, cooking for **2 minutes per side** until golden.
3. Stack pancakes, layering with strawberries and whipped cream, then drizzle with syrup.

Chef's Tips: Use room-temperature strawberries for better flavor.
Notes: Swap maple syrup for honey for a different sweetness.

Buffalo Soldier Super Bowl Buffalo Chicken Nachos

Prep Time: 10 minutes | **Cook Time:** 8 minutes | **Total Time:** 18 minutes

Ingredients
Main Ingredients:
- ½ pound cooked shredded chicken
- 2 cups tortilla chips
- ¼ cup shredded cheddar cheese

Seasonings & Sauces:
- ½ teaspoon salt
- ¼ teaspoon black pepper
- 2 tablespoons buffalo sauce
- 1 tablespoon ranch dressing

Optional Additions:
- 1 teaspoon chopped jalapeños
- ½ teaspoon smoked paprika for extra flavor

Nutritional Information
- **Calories:** 580 kcal
- **Carbs:** 48g
- **Fiber:** 4g
- **Protein:** 38g
- **Fats:** 24g
- **Sugar:** 6g

Instructions
1. **Preheat the Blackstone Griddle** to **medium heat** and warm the shredded chicken.
2. Spread tortilla chips on the griddle, then layer with chicken, cheese, and buffalo sauce.
3. Cover with a melting dome for **3 minutes**, then drizzle with ranch dressing before serving.

Chef's Tips: Use a cast-iron skillet on the griddle for crispier nachos.
Notes: Swap cheddar for Monterey Jack for a creamier melt.

Southern Glory Mardi Gras Cajun Shrimp & Grits

Prep Time: 10 minutes | **Cook Time:** 10 minutes | **Total Time:** 20 minutes

Ingredients
Main Ingredients:
- ½ pound large shrimp, peeled and deveined
- 1 cup cooked grits
- 1 tablespoon unsalted butter

Seasonings & Sauces:
- ½ teaspoon salt
- ¼ teaspoon black pepper
- ½ teaspoon Cajun seasoning
- 1 teaspoon fresh lemon juice

Optional Additions:
- 1 teaspoon chopped green onions
- ½ teaspoon hot sauce for spice

Nutritional Information
- **Calories:** 520 kcal
- **Carbs:** 45g
- **Fiber:** 3g
- **Protein:** 36g
- **Fats:** 22g
- **Sugar:** 4g

Instructions
1. **Preheat the Blackstone Griddle** to **medium-high heat** and lightly oil the surface.
2. Toss shrimp with salt, black pepper, and Cajun seasoning, then cook for **3–4 minutes per side**.
3. Plate shrimp over warm grits, drizzle with melted butter and lemon juice.

Chef's Tips: Use stone-ground grits for a richer texture.
Notes: Swap Cajun seasoning for Old Bay for a milder spice.

Westward Ho' Halloween Spooky Smash Burgers

P rep Time: 10 minutes | **Cook Time:** 8 minutes | **Total Time:** 18 minutes

Ingredients
Main Ingredients:
- ½ pound ground beef (80/20)
- 2 black sesame seed burger buns
- 2 slices sharp cheddar cheese (cut into jack-o'-lantern shapes)
- 2 slices crispy bacon

Seasonings & Sauces:
- ½ teaspoon salt
- ¼ teaspoon black pepper
- ½ teaspoon garlic powder
- 1 tablespoon spicy mayo

Optional Additions:
- 1 teaspoon hot sauce for extra heat
- 1 teaspoon caramelized onions for added flavor

Nutritional Information
- **Calories:** 720 kcal
- **Carbs:** 42g
- **Fiber:** 3g
- **Protein:** 48g
- **Fats:** 38g
- **Sugar:** 5g

Instructions
1. **Preheat the Blackstone Griddle** to **medium-high heat** and toast buns.
2. Form beef into two balls and smash onto the griddle, pressing firmly for crispy edges.
3. Cook for **2–3 minutes per side**, flipping once, then add cheese.
4. Stack burgers with bacon and spicy mayo, then serve on spooky-themed buns.

Chef's Tips: Cut cheese into ghost or pumpkin shapes for a fun Halloween theme.
Notes: Use pretzel buns for a different spooky effect.

The Founding Fathers' Labor Day Grilled Sausage & Peppers

Prep Time: 10 minutes | **Cook Time:** 12 minutes | **Total Time:** 22 minutes

Ingredients
Main Ingredients:
- 2 Italian sausages
- 1 small onion, sliced
- 1 small red bell pepper, sliced
- 2 hoagie rolls

Seasonings & Sauces:
- ½ teaspoon salt
- ¼ teaspoon black pepper
- ½ teaspoon garlic powder
- 1 tablespoon Dijon mustard

Optional Additions:
- 1 teaspoon Worcestershire sauce for depth
- ½ teaspoon red pepper flakes for spice

Nutritional Information
- **Calories:** 680 kcal
- **Carbs:** 45g
- **Fiber:** 4g
- **Protein:** 38g
- **Fats:** 36g
- **Sugar:** 6g

Instructions
1. **Preheat the Blackstone Griddle** to **medium heat** and cook sausages for **5–6 minutes per side**.
2. Sauté onions and peppers for **6 minutes**, stirring occasionally.
3. Toast hoagie rolls, then assemble with sausages, sautéed vegetables, and Dijon mustard.

Chef's Tips: Cook sausages under a melting dome for even heating.
Notes: Swap Italian sausages for bratwurst for a German-style twist.

Freedom Christmas Eve Griddled Seafood Feast

Prep Time: 15 minutes | **Cook Time:** 12 minutes | **Total Time:** 27 minutes

Ingredients
Main Ingredients:
- 4 large sea scallops
- 4 jumbo shrimp, peeled and deveined
- 2 small lobster tails, split in half

Seasonings & Sauces:
- ½ teaspoon salt
- ¼ teaspoon black pepper
- ½ teaspoon garlic powder
- ½ teaspoon smoked paprika
- 1 tablespoon melted butter

Optional Additions:
- 1 teaspoon lemon zest
- ½ teaspoon fresh parsley for garnish

Nutritional Information
- **Calories:** 580 kcal
- **Carbs:** 4g
- **Fiber:** 0g
- **Protein:** 54g
- **Fats:** 36g
- **Sugar:** 1g

Instructions
1. **Preheat the Blackstone Griddle** to **medium heat** and lightly oil the surface.
2. Season seafood with salt, pepper, garlic powder, and smoked paprika.
3. Cook scallops and shrimp for **2–3 minutes per side**, then lobster for **5–6 minutes**.
4. Baste with melted butter and garnish with lemon zest and parsley.

Chef's Tips: Use a griddle press for better seafood caramelization.
Notes: Swap lobster for king crab legs for a luxurious touch.

Patriot-Style Veteran's Day Smoked Brisket Plate

Prep Time: 10 minutes | **Cook Time:** 10 minutes | **Total Time:** 20 minutes

Ingredients
Main Ingredients:
- ½ pound smoked brisket, sliced
- 1 small cornbread muffin
- ¼ cup coleslaw

Seasonings & Sauces:
- ½ teaspoon salt
- ¼ teaspoon black pepper
- ½ teaspoon BBQ rub
- 2 tablespoons BBQ sauce

Optional Additions:
- ½ teaspoon cayenne for spice
- 1 teaspoon honey for sweetness

Nutritional Information
- **Calories:** 700 kcal
- **Carbs:** 45g
- **Fiber:** 3g
- **Protein:** 48g
- **Fats:** 34g
- **Sugar:** 10g

Instructions
1. **Preheat the Blackstone Griddle** to **medium heat** and warm brisket for **5 minutes**, flipping once.
2. Toast cornbread on the griddle, then serve with brisket, coleslaw, and BBQ sauce.

Chef's Tips: Let brisket rest before slicing for juicier meat.
Notes: Swap cornbread for Texas toast for a classic BBQ plate.

Red, White & Blueberry 4th of July Flag Cake

Prep Time: 15 minutes | **Cook Time:** 8 minutes | **Total Time:** 23 minutes

Ingredients
Main Ingredients:
- 1 cup pancake batter
- ¼ cup fresh blueberries
- ¼ cup sliced strawberries
- ¼ cup whipped cream

Seasonings & Sauces:
- ½ teaspoon vanilla extract
- 1 tablespoon maple syrup
- 1 teaspoon powdered sugar

Optional Additions:
- ½ teaspoon cinnamon for warmth
- 1 tablespoon crushed pecans for crunch

Nutritional Information
- **Calories:** 480 kcal
- **Carbs:** 65g
- **Fiber:** 5g
- **Protein:** 12g
- **Fats:** 14g
- **Sugar:** 20g

Instructions
1. **Preheat the Blackstone Griddle** to **medium heat** and lightly butter the surface.
2. Pour pancake batter into a rectangle, then arrange blueberries and strawberries in a flag pattern.
3. Cook for **3 minutes per side**, then top with whipped cream and powdered sugar.

Chef's Tips: Use a cookie cutter to shape pancakes into stars for extra festivity.
Notes: Swap maple syrup for honey for a different sweetness.

CHAPTER 9: ADVANCED TIPS & TRICKS

Mastering a **Blackstone Griddle** goes beyond basic cooking—it's about refining techniques that maximize flavor, texture, and consistency. Perfecting the crisp on any dish, balancing spice combinations for bold, layered flavors, and ensuring even cooking without burning all require precision. These advanced methods separate ordinary meals from restaurant-quality results, turning every cook into a true griddle expert.

How to Get the Perfect Crisp on Everything

Crispness isn't just about high heat—it's about understanding how moisture, surface contact, and fat interact with food. A perfectly crisp exterior doesn't happen by accident; it's a balance of technique, timing, and precise temperature control. Whether you're making golden hash browns, a deeply caramelized crust on a steak, or crackling bacon with just the right amount of crunch, the key is knowing how to manipulate heat and ingredients to your advantage.

Moisture is the biggest enemy of crispness. If too much water remains on the surface of food when it hits the griddle, the first thing that happens isn't browning—it's steaming. That's why drying ingredients properly is essential. Proteins like chicken and steak should be **patted completely dry** with a paper towel before cooking, removing excess surface moisture that would otherwise interfere with browning. Vegetables need to be washed ahead of time and dried thoroughly, especially if they contain a high water content like zucchini or mushrooms. Even potatoes, when used for fries or hash browns, benefit from an additional step: soaking them in cold water for at least 30 minutes, then drying them completely before cooking. This removes excess starch, which can cause uneven crisping and make the texture gummy rather than crunchy.

Surface contact is just as critical. A griddle provides a large, even surface to cook on, but that doesn't mean food should be moved constantly. A proper crisp needs **direct, uninterrupted contact with the hot steel**. Constant flipping or stirring prevents the exterior from developing a crust, leading to food that's browned but never truly crispy. When making smash burgers, the key is pressing them down firmly and letting them cook undisturbed until a deep crust forms. Hash browns should be spread in a thin, even layer and left alone for several minutes before flipping. Patience is what makes the difference between a soft, steamed texture and a crisp, golden crunch.

Fat plays a major role in crisping, but using the right amount is key. Too much oil can cause food to fry rather than sear, leading to a greasy texture instead of a structured crisp. Too little oil results in uneven browning and food that sticks. The trick is **coating the surface lightly and evenly**, ensuring the food has just enough fat to conduct heat while maintaining structure. Oils with a high smoke point, such as avocado or canola oil, perform best for crisping since they won't burn or break down under high temperatures. Butter can be used for flavor, but it should always be added at the end of cooking to prevent scorching.

Temperature control separates crisp perfection from burnt disaster. A griddle that's too hot burns the outside before the inside is cooked, while too low of a temperature creates a limp, soggy texture. Adjusting heat zones allows for **searing at high temperatures** before transferring food to a slightly cooler area to finish cooking. This prevents the risk of overcooking while ensuring the texture stays crisp and satisfying.

Mastering the art of crisping isn't just about cooking at high heat—it's about understanding how ingredients react to moisture, fat, and direct contact. When executed correctly, crispness isn't just a texture—it's the defining feature of a perfectly cooked dish.

Spice Combinations to Elevate Every Dish

A perfectly cooked meal on the **Blackstone Griddle** is only as good as the seasoning behind it. Heat and technique bring out texture, but the right blend of spices transforms food from basic to bold. Cooking without understanding seasoning is like painting without color—it works, but it lacks depth. Spices don't just add heat or aroma; they create contrast, balance, and complexity that can make a dish unforgettable.

Layering flavors is the foundation of great seasoning. A single spice rarely does the job alone. The best combinations create depth, blending heat, sweetness, smokiness, or umami in a way that enhances rather than overwhelms. Salt is always the starting point. It doesn't just make food salty—it unlocks natural flavors, drawing out moisture and intensifying everything it touches. Kosher salt or sea salt performs better than table salt, sticking to the surface of meats and vegetables while allowing other seasonings to adhere properly. Without it, spices sit on the surface without integrating fully into the dish.

A well-balanced spice blend follows a simple principle: contrast drives flavor. If there's heat, there should be sweetness. If there's richness, there should be acidity. A smoky, grilled steak becomes richer with the deep warmth of paprika or cayenne, but adding a touch of brown sugar or coffee powder rounds out the intensity with a subtle, caramelized finish. The same concept applies to chicken—garlic and onion powder provide a strong, savory backbone, but the addition of a citrus zest or smoked cumin cuts through the richness, keeping it from feeling too heavy.

Spice blends should be built with the specific cooking process in mind. High-heat griddling requires **bold flavors that can withstand searing temperatures**. Delicate spices like basil or parsley lose their essence when exposed to direct heat, while heartier ones—smoked paprika, chipotle powder, coriander—develop richer flavors as they cook. Some spices need fat to unlock their full potential. Black pepper, for example, becomes more fragrant when mixed with oil before being applied to meat, while mustard powder intensifies when combined with vinegar or citrus juice.

Timing matters. Seasoning too early on a high-heat griddle can lead to burning, especially with sugar-based rubs or fine powders that char too quickly. A spice blend with brown sugar, for instance, should be applied only in the final moments of cooking, allowing it to caramelize without turning bitter. On the other hand, bold, earthy flavors—like a mix of smoked paprika, cumin, and cracked black pepper—thrive when added early, allowing them to fuse with the surface of a steak or burger.

Pre-made spice blends can work, but they rarely match the impact of **a fresh, carefully curated mix**. Toasting whole spices before grinding them intensifies their potency, while making a small batch ensures freshness rather than relying on stale store-bought versions. The best cooks don't just throw seasonings on their food; they understand how each element interacts, creating balance in every bite. When seasoning is done right, it doesn't just enhance flavor—it defines the entire dish.

Techniques for Even Cooking & Avoiding Burnt Food

Cooking on a **Blackstone Griddle** is all about control. Without the right approach, food burns too fast, cooks unevenly, or comes off the surface half-raw in some spots and overdone in others. Heat moves differently on a griddle than it does in a pan or over an open flame, so knowing how to manage it is the difference between frustration and perfection. Every well-cooked dish starts with understanding **how heat transfers, how food reacts, and how to adjust techniques in real time**.

Heat doesn't stay still—it spreads. A griddle's burners concentrate heat in specific areas, but the steel surface **absorbs and radiates that heat outward**. The section directly above a burner will always be hotter, while edges and corners tend to run cooler. This natural temperature variation is an advantage when used correctly, allowing for **high-heat searing, medium-heat cooking, and low-heat holding zones**. Food should never be placed randomly on the griddle—each ingredient needs to be positioned based on how much heat it requires and how long it needs to cook. A thick-cut steak should start in the hottest zone for a hard sear, then be moved to a cooler section to finish without burning. Pancakes need steady, even heat, so they belong in a medium zone where they can cook through without scorching.

Patience separates burned food from properly cooked food. The instinct to constantly flip or move ingredients works against even cooking. Food needs **consistent contact with the surface** to develop the right texture. A smash burger left undisturbed for the first minute forms the deep brown crust that defines it. Hash browns that sit in place for several minutes crisp up properly, while those that are moved too soon break apart and steam rather than fry. A common mistake is pressing food down at the wrong time—smashing a burger once during the initial sear enhances browning, but doing it after juices have started escaping **forces moisture out, drying the meat instead of locking in flavor**.

Layering ingredients at the wrong moment causes imbalances in cooking. A cheeseburger topped with onions too early will trap steam under the cheese, turning it mushy rather than letting it caramelize. When making a stir-fry, denser vegetables like carrots or broccoli need to hit the surface first, while delicate ones like bell peppers or bean sprouts should be added later to avoid overcooking. Timing matters just as much as placement, ensuring that all elements finish cooking together rather than having some ingredients overdone while others are still raw.

Heat management also extends to oil usage. Too much oil pools on the surface, frying rather than searing food and preventing proper caramelization. Too little oil leads to sticking, making it difficult to lift and flip delicate ingredients like eggs or fish. The right balance depends on the food—enough oil to coat the surface without excess buildup. Spreading it with a spatula or using a squeeze bottle provides **an even layer that enhances browning while maintaining control**.

Great griddle cooking isn't just about heat—it's about control, timing, and knowing how ingredients react on the surface. The right crisp, the perfect seasoning balance, and precise heat management transform simple ingredients into unforgettable dishes. Mastering these techniques means every meal reaches its full potential, delivering consistently flawless results every time.

CHAPTER 10: MEASUREMENT CONVERSIONS

Precision in cooking is key to achieving consistent, delicious results. Whether you're scaling a recipe, converting temperatures, or adjusting ingredient measurements, understanding unit conversions ensures accuracy. With the Blackstone Griddle, knowing the right ratios between U.S. and metric units helps streamline the cooking process for beginners and experienced grillers alike.

U.S. to Metric Unit Conversions

U.S. Unit	Metric Equivalent
1 teaspoon (tsp)	4.93 mL
1 tablespoon (tbsp)	14.79 mL
1 fluid ounce (fl oz)	29.57 mL
1 cup	236.59 mL
1 pint (pt)	473.18 mL
1 quart (qt)	946.35 mL
1 gallon (gal)	3.79 L
1 ounce (oz)	28.35 g
1 pound (lb)	0.45 kg
1 inch (in)	2.54 cm

Temperature Conversion Chart (Fahrenheit to Celsius)

Fahrenheit (°F)	Celsius (°C)
32	0.0
50	10.0
100	37.77777777777778
150	65.55555555555556
200	93.33333333333333
250	121.11111111111111
300	148.88888888888889
350	176.66666666666666
400	204.44444444444446
450	232.2222222222223

	500	260.0

Weight & Volume Equivalents: Tablespoons to Ounces & Grams

Teaspoons (tsp)	Ounces (oz)	Grams (g)
1	0.16666666666666666	4.93
2	0.3333333333333333	9.86
3	0.5	14.79
4	0.6666666666666666	19.72
5	0.8333333333333334	24.65

Mastering measurement conversions eliminates guesswork, making it easier to follow recipes and experiment confidently. Whether adjusting temperatures, portion sizes, or ingredient weights, these conversions equip you with the knowledge to cook efficiently on your Blackstone Griddle every time.

CONCLUSION

Cooking on a Blackstone Griddle means developing a range of skills that improve over time. Every cook, every adjustment, and every new technique refines the way food is prepared, leading to better flavors, textures, and consistency. The journey doesn't stop at mastering the basics; it evolves with every griddle session, pushing the limits of creativity and precision.

Your Blackstone Journey: What You've Learned

Cooking on a **Blackstone Griddle** is more than just preparing food—it's about control, technique, and an evolving understanding of how heat, surface contact, and seasoning shape every meal. From the first time the burners ignite to the moment a perfectly seared steak or golden-brown pancake leaves the griddle, the process is one of **continuous refinement**. Mastering this craft isn't just about following steps; it's about developing instincts that turn simple cooking into something remarkable.

Every meal cooked on the griddle builds a deeper connection between the cook and the surface. The first time food is placed down, the immediate sizzle sets the tone—too hot, and it burns before it can cook through, too cool, and it struggles to develop the right sear. The rhythm of cooking becomes second nature over time, knowing when to leave food undisturbed to build crust, when to shift it to a lower heat zone, and when a slight adjustment in oil can mean the difference between crisp and soggy. Each session teaches the nuances of heat distribution, where the strongest searing points exist, and how to use those zones to execute a dish flawlessly.

Mistakes become lessons that shape future cooks. A burger flipped too soon without letting the crust develop, hash browns that steam instead of crisping, or chicken that's overcooked on the outside and raw inside—these experiences sharpen awareness, making adjustments more intuitive with every meal. Cooking on a griddle isn't about perfection from the start; it's about **paying attention to the small details that improve results with each use**. The seasoning of the surface evolves the same way, transforming from a thin, fragile layer into a durable, naturally non-stick cooking base. With every session, the griddle becomes more seasoned, more reliable, and more capable of handling anything thrown onto it.

Cooking transforms when seasoning isn't just about adding salt, but understanding how flavors work together to enhance natural ingredients. Balancing heat, acidity, and depth in spice combinations becomes instinctive, allowing food to be elevated beyond the ordinary. The power of contrast—sweet and smoky, spicy and rich—turns standard dishes into **bold, unforgettable flavors**. Over time, spice blends become second nature, customized to personal preferences and perfected through experience.

A well-used Blackstone tells a story. The seasoned steel, darkened over time, reflects every meal that's been cooked on it. The slight imperfections in the surface—marks left from a high-heat sear or the gradual build-up of a well-maintained cooking patina—aren't flaws; they're proof of experience. The griddle evolves alongside the cook, getting better with each use, just as the person cooking on it sharpens their technique with every meal.

Cooking on a Blackstone is more than a skill—it's a craft, a process that turns an ordinary flat-top into an extension of the cook's knowledge, instincts, and experience. With every meal, there's an opportunity to **refine, improve, and elevate the cooking process**, making the journey as rewarding as the food itself.

How to Keep Improving Your Griddle Skills

Mastering a **Blackstone Griddle** isn't a one-time achievement—it's an evolving skill that sharpens with every cook. No matter how many meals have been made, there's always room to refine techniques, push flavors further, and gain a deeper understanding of how the griddle responds under different conditions. The difference between a good cook and a great one isn't just knowledge, but the ability to **observe, adjust, and improve with every use**.

Cooking on a griddle is a **real-time experience**, requiring awareness of how heat interacts with food at every stage. A steak doesn't just sear—it reacts to temperature, oil, and seasoning in ways that change throughout the cooking process. Learning to recognize those cues—when the surface is just hot enough for the perfect crust, when an ingredient is ready to be flipped, or when a dish needs an extra second to finish—separates someone who simply follows steps from someone who truly understands the griddle. The more time spent cooking, the stronger that instinct becomes, turning hesitation into confidence and repetition into mastery.

Experimentation fuels progress. Sticking to the same routine produces familiar results, but stepping outside of that comfort zone unlocks new possibilities. Adjusting cooking temperatures slightly, layering spices differently, or testing a new technique forces a deeper connection with the process. A slight shift in timing can mean the difference between a good crust and a flawless one, between a well-cooked meal and something that tastes restaurant-level. Testing different cuts of meat, trying new oils, or introducing unexpected ingredients pushes boundaries, turning what was once routine into something dynamic.

Observation isn't just about food—it's about understanding the **griddle itself**. Each session leaves small signs of how heat moves, how seasoning builds, and how food reacts to the steel surface. Identifying these subtle details—whether it's recognizing where the hottest zones develop, knowing how the surface changes over time, or adjusting seasoning methods—refines not only technique but also control. The griddle isn't just a tool; it's a surface that evolves with use, and the best cooks learn to read it like a well-worn recipe.

Precision comes with repetition. The perfect pancake flip, the exact moment a burger reaches peak juiciness, the way vegetables caramelize at just the right speed—none of these happen by accident. They are the result of accumulated experience, of learning from small missteps, of refining movements until they become second nature. Cooking isn't about perfection from the start—it's about continuous improvement, **small adjustments that add up over time** until every move, every seasoning choice, and every heat adjustment feels effortless.

Great griddle cooking isn't about reaching a finish line—it's about constantly learning, adjusting, and improving. Every meal is an opportunity to refine techniques, experiment with flavors, and build instinctive control over heat and timing. The best cooks aren't just experienced; they're always looking for ways to make their next dish even better.